dig, plant, grow

Love & Wishes —
Have fun
[signature]
12-04

Published by Cool Springs Press, a Division of Thomas Nelson, Inc.
P.O. Box 141000, Nashville, Tennessee 37214.

Rushing, Felder, 1952-
   Dig, plant, grow : a kid's guide to gardening / Felder Rushing.
      p. cm.
   1. Gardening—Juvenile literature. I. Title.
   SB457.F869 2004
   635—dc22

                                   2004013046

ISBN: 1-59186-093-8

First printing 2004
Printed in the United States of America
10 9 8 7 6 5 4 3 2 1

Managing Editor: Jenny Andrews
Designer: Bill Kersey
Production Artist: S. E. Anderson

Visit www.ThomasNelson.com or www.coolspringspress.net

Photo Credits

Photos are by **Felder Rushing** unless listed otherwise below.

Thomas Eltzroth: 74AB, 76A, 77A, 78A, 80AB, 85AB, 86AB, 87B, 88AB, 89AB, 90AB, 91AB, 94B, 95A, 96AB, 97AB, 98AB, 101AB, 102A, 103B, 107A, 108B, 109A, 111B, 112B, 113B, 115B, 118B, 120A, 122AB, 124B, 127A, 128B, 129A, 131A, 135A

Jerry Pavia: 34A, 75B, 76B, 77B, 79AB, 82B, 94A, 102B, 107B, 110A, 112A, 114AB, 119A, 120B, 121AB, 130A, 133, 135B, 137A

Liz Ball: 78B, 82A, 104B, 117, 118A, 123AB, 137B

André Viette: 108A

Ralph Snodsmith: 119B

Key: A=top photo, B=bottom photo

dig, plant, grow

A Kid's Guide to Gardening

Felder Rushing

COOL SPRINGS PRESS
A Division of Thomas Nelson Publishers
Since 1798

www.thomasnelson.com

Acknowledgements

The author wishes to credit the generous assistance of the staff at the American Horticultural Society, members of the National Youth Gardening Advisory Committee from all over the country, staffs at botanical gardens from coast to coast, children's library librarians, Master Gardeners, and many dozens of kids—particularly the 4-H PLANT CAMP KIDS OF DESOTO COUNTY, MISSISSIPPI—who put the projects together.

I am especially grateful for the guidance of Dr. John Guyton, a uniquely motivated, highly energized 4-H Environmental Education specialist, who in 2003 was doubly honored as both the National Project Learning Tree Outstanding Educator, and the AHS Great American Gardeners Teacher of the Year. His ability to pull cool stuff out of his pockets—including a "pocket terrarium" made from a clear film canister stuffed with moss—to capture the imagination of kids and adults alike, helped inspire this book.

Felder Rushing

Table of Contents

List of Projects

Getting Started

IN THIS BOOK there are lots of fun projects to do, and interesting plants to learn about. And there are some tips in the back for grownups on how to use gardening to explore and learn. You can also DISCOVER:

- Parts of a plant
- Words gardeners use
- What and where plants need to grow
- Good tools to use
- How to make good soil out of plain dirt
- How to choose and grow easy flowers
- Art projects to make your garden fun
- How to attract birds to your garden
- Plus, you will have FUN—and can share what you learn with others.

Safety First

NOBODY likes RULES, but some you NEED to know. Have FUN, but BE CAREFUL!

SHARP STUFF CAN CUT YOU—Be sure you get help when you have to pick up heavy things, when you need to use scissors or a knife to cut things, when you need to climb a ladder, and when you need to use something hot like an oven. And watch your fingers when using a hammer or hot glue gun.

SOME THINGS STING—Never, ever try to catch a bee or spider by yourself, even with a jar.

SOME PLANTS ARE POISONOUS—There are some very pretty berries that birds can eat, but these berries can make you sick if you eat them. Be very careful what you eat out of a garden—some plants have chemicals in them that are poisonous to humans! And don't stick berries in your ear or nose, or they may get stuck.

THE SUN CAN BURN YOU—Wear a hat and put on sunscreen if you will be outside for a long time.

GROWNUPS CAN GET MAD—Always clean up when you finish a project.

LEARN TO USE GARDEN TOOLS—Get a grownup to show you how to use tools and how to take care of them, and don't use them for throwing or hitting.

THE INTERNET HAS LOTS OF INFORMATION—There are some cool gardening sites for kids, but bad things can pop up when you least expect them. Tell a grownup if something shows up that makes you uncomfortable.

Plant Parts

ROOTS grow in the ground and find water and plant food, and hold the plant up. STEMS and BRANCHES are above the ground and hold LEAVES out where they can catch sunshine to turn into plant energy. FLOWERS make SEEDS or FRUIT, with the help of butterflies, bees, and even the wind to spread their dusty pollen.

We love to look at, touch, and smell plants. We can even EAT some of them.

- Carrots are roots.
- Celery is a stem.
- Lettuce is a leaf.
- Broccoli is a bunch of little flowers.
- Sunflowers make seeds to eat.
- Grapes are little fruits called berries.
- Can you name more plant parts we can eat?

Each PART plays an important role in the life and health of the plant. And the way the parts are arranged, their color and shape, how they feel and smell can help us IDENTIFY the plant and understand it better.

Words Gardeners Use

People who cook use special cooking words. Gardeners use gardening words. Some are very easy, and others take a little time to learn. Here are a few that can help you ask for things you need, or you can use them to tell other people about your garden.

Annual: Plant that lives only part of the year

Bulb: Fat underground part of some plants

Compost: Dark crumbly stuff made from old leaves and kitchen scraps

Container: A pot that holds soil for growing plants, with a hole to let water out

Fertilizer: Plant food that we buy at the garden store or make from compost

Flowers: Pretty parts of a plant that make seeds and fruit and attract butterflies, bees, and other insects

Frost: The white stuff that comes in cold weather that is not snow or ice

Fruit: The part of a plant that has seeds and can sometimes be eaten

Full sun: Where there is no shade most of the day

Grass: Little flat-growing plants with thin leaves that we can walk and play on

Hose: Long rubber tube that carries water

Labyrinth: A walk-through garden area that leads to the center, and back out again (does not have choices to make like a maze)

Lawn: The big area of grass you play on and bigger kids or grownups mow

Leaves: Part of the plant that turns sunlight into plant energy

Maze: A walk-through puzzle made with plants or other things, where you have to make choices about which direction to go to get to the other side

Mulch: A layer or blanket of leaves or compost on top of the soil, keeps roots cool

Part shade: Shade part of the day, and sun part of the day

Perennial: A plant that lives for several years

Potting soil: Soil you buy at a garden store to grow plants in containers

Roots: Underground plant parts that hold the plant up and absorb water and plant food

Season: Winter, spring, summer, and fall

Seed: Part of the plant that grows into a new plant, some can be eaten, others cannot

Shade: No sun most of the day

Shrub: A plant with hard stems that gets big and lives for many years

Soil: What plants grow in, some people call it dirt

Stake: A tall stick or pole you can tie tall plants or vines onto

Stem: Part of a plant that holds leaves and flowers up toward the sun

Thorn: Sharp part growing on cactus and the stems of roses and other plants

Tools: Things you can use to garden, like a shovel, rake, and hose

Vegetable: Plant you can eat part of

Vine: A plant with long stems that needs to climb on something

Weed: A plant growing where you don't want it to grow

Good Tools

Gardeners use their favorite tools a lot. Here are some good ones.

Bucket: Carries soil, water, and tools, can be used to sit on

Gloves: Keeps thorns and dirt off of your hands

Hose: Brings water to the garden from a water faucet

Notebook and pen or pencil: Helps you keep notes and draw

Pots: Come in lots of sizes for growing different plants

Potting soil: Helps grow plants in containers

Pruning shears: Short, sharp garden scissors

Rake: Helps make the soil smooth before planting

Ruler: Helps measure

Shovel: Helps you dig in the soil

String or twine: Ties plants and vines to stakes or fences

Trowel: A little shovel you can use for planting

Watering can: Helps take water to potted plants inside and out

Where Do You Garden?

Our country is very large, and has LOTS of different kinds of weather and soils. Some places have short gardening seasons, and long cold winters. Others have long, hot summers and rainy winters. In some places you can garden nearly ALL YEAR.

Many people live where it gets COLD in the winter, and plants take a break from growing. While there are plenty of fun activities to do during the winter and

plants that grow indoors, there are some things you can do to make the out-doors more interesting. You can create your own GARDEN ORNAMENTS, and containers can be pretty and colorful, even without plants!

Make a MAP of your state, and see what kind of weath-er there is each month. When does it get the coldest? The hottest? What month gets the most rain? The least?

Where Can You Get Plants?

A grownup that gardens can help you choose the best plants from this book for growing in your area. Visit a GARDEN STORE in the spring to see what you can grow in the spring and summer, and visit it again in the fall to see what grows best during the fall and winter. A garden center can have LOTS of fun ideas that don't cost much money.

Many gardeners are happy to SHARE PLANTS from their gardens and will give you cuttings or divisions or seeds. Only take a plant (or piece of a plant) from a garden if the GARDENER gives you permission or has offered it to you as a gift. Get to know gardeners who are friends of your parents, or who live nearby—they can TEACH you a lot about plants and nature. And you can share plants with them, too. There might even be great gardeners in your own FAMILY.

Wildlife in the Garden

We share the world with other creatures, from good guys like BUTTERFLIES and LADYBUGS, to some that can be a little grouchy. Wasps and spiders are good for the garden, but they can bite or sting if you scare them or mistreat them. Even a bird will try to bite if you pick it up!

Caterpillars may eat your plants, but they grow up into beautiful butterflies and moths. And even things that can hurt you can be good for the garden— without BEES, some flowers could not make seeds. And SPIDERS eat bugs that are eating your garden. So, always  be careful around all kinds of WILDLIFE—never kill something just because you are bigger or are scared of it! See if a grownup can help make it leave, or move it to a better place.

If something is hurting you or your garden—like mosquitoes, slugs and snails, beetles, and maybe even a snake—then see if there is an easy, natural way to control it without using grownup poisons that may not be good for you or your garden. Remember, the garden is a little piece of the WHOLE WORLD, and it should be a place of WELCOME to all creatures.

Be Creative

The FUN projects and plants in this book are only a few of the ways you can be creative in the garden. PLANT some stuff in the spring and summer, and try a few plants in the fall and winter, too. Be on the lookout for GOOD IDEAS from other people and places. And you can also come up with your own ideas. You can use all sorts of MATERIALS, even "trash" like empty soda bottles, cans, and milk jugs—think of it as another way to RECYCLE! It can be as complicated as building a dinosaur sculpture, or as simple as making a clothespin butterfly.

There are LOTS of plants and ideas in this book, but don't worry about growing or doing them all—just have fun, take your time, and you will be surprised at what you LEARN along the way. And share what you learn with others! They might have something interesting to teach you, too!

Easy Projects

FUN THINGS to do, like making and building stuff, are sometimes called "projects" by grownups. Here are a few IDEAS, including things that will help your garden GROW, ways to get more birds and butterflies to visit, and instructions on making better dirt using recycled kitchen scraps.

None of these projects is very hard to do, but you MIGHT need a little help with some of them—when using a knife, scissors, or a saw, or if you need to buy the kind of paint that will last a long time outdoors, you may need to ask a grownup to help.

Remember These Rules:

- Always be careful.
- Always clean up any mess you make.
- Get a grownup or older kid to help you with sharp tools and really heavy things.

Some projects can be done in a lot of different ways. Read the directions and LOOK AT THE PICTURES. If you don't understand the instructions or if you have questions, ask an older kid or a grownup.

The important thing is HAVE FUN!

Milk Jug Bird Feeder

Recycle a plastic milk jug into a pretty bird feeder.

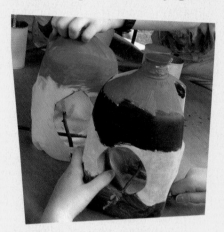

What You NEED:
- One-gallon plastic milk jug
- Scissors
- Piece of wire
- Two pencil-thick sticks
- Paint
- Birdseed

What to DO:
1. Cut big holes in the sides of the milk jug.
2. Punch four little holes near the bottom and slide the sticks through for bird perches. Punch a couple of holes near the top for the wire.
3. Paint the jugs.
4. Put birdseed in the bottom. Hang it from a branch of a tree using the piece of wire.

Try This

Different kinds of birds eat all sorts of seeds, berries, fruit, and insects, but you can attract many types of birds using just sunflower seeds.

Coffee Can Birdhouse

Birds like cool places to make nests. Make one and decorate it with natural twigs. "Bee" careful—wasps sometimes like to nest in birdhouses!

What You NEED:
- Coffee can with plastic lid
- Hammer and nail
- Wire
- Scissors
- Lots of pencil-sized twigs
- Rubber bands

What to DO:
1. Cut a hole near one side of the coffee can lid large enough for a bird.
2. Punch a hole in the bottom of the coffee can using the hammer and nail.
3. Snap on the plastic lid, with the bird hole lined up with the hole in the can bottom.
4. Use rubber bands to hold twigs all the way around the can to make it look natural.
5. Add a longer twig for a perch.
6. Run the wire through the hole in the can and the hole in the lid, to hang it up in a tree.

Terrarium

This is an easy way to have your very own miniature tropical garden—or even a desert—without having to go outside your own home. Make your little garden in a big plastic sweater box, and give the plants the right amounts of water and sunlight.

What you NEED:

- Big plastic sweater box or old glass aquarium
- Clean gravel
- Potting soil (and sand if you're making a desert)
- Little plants
- Bulb baster

Try This

Jungle plants need more water than desert plants, so if you make a desert terrarium let the plants dry out between watering times.

What to DO:

❶ Pour a layer of clean gravel one inch deep.

❷ Spread a layer of potting soil about four inches deep.

❸ Carefully loosen roots of little plants, and plant them in the potting soil.

❹ Add small toy lizards or other creatures.

❺ Water the plants slowly.

❻ Use the bulb baster to soak up extra water from beneath the gravel so plants won't be sitting in too much water.

❼ Keep your terrarium near a bright window, but not directly in the sunlight.

Sand Art Votive

Special times in the garden can use a little light—and you can make your own luminary! Remember not to leave the jar outside all the time or it can fill up with rainwater. And get a grownup to help you light the candle.

What You NEED:
- Clear glass jar
- Colored sand
- Small paintbrush
- Votive candle

What to DO:
1. Pour a little colored sand in the jar, then add another layer of a different color, then another and another.
2. Use the paintbrush to smooth out the layers, and to push around the edges of the jar to make patterns in the sand.
3. Carefully add the candle.

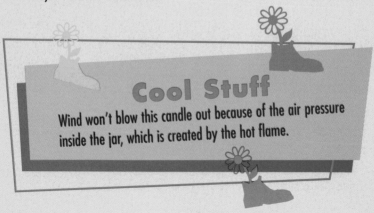

Cool Stuff
Wind won't blow this candle out because of the air pressure inside the jar, which is created by the hot flame.

Cool Stuff

Sound is caused by vibrations in the air. With wind chimes, not only can you hear the wind, you can see it as well.

Aluminum Can Chimes

Some sounds are pretty and some are just noisy, but they are all still sounds! Wind chimes can be made out of metal, pottery, or glass. You can make a fun one from old cola cans.

What you NEED:

- Five or six cans
- String
- Foot-long sticks
- Hammer and nail

What to DO:

❶ Punch holes in the bottoms of the cans with the hammer and nail.
❷ Cut pieces of string.
❸ Tie a big knot in the end of each piece of string and pull the strings through the cans.
❹ Tie the sticks together and tie the cans to the sticks.
❺ Hang outside.

Plants in Pots

Wild plants grow in the ground in just plain dirt and a lot of good garden plants do, too. But many gardeners also like to grow plants in pots. Plastic pots or clay pots are the easiest to use because they already have holes in the bottoms for extra water to drain out.

You can make your own pots out of nearly anything that holds soil—old shoes, tires, wheelbarrows, big cans, wooden boxes, paint buckets, cooking pots, an old hat, or even just a bag of potting soil.

What you NEED:

- Anything that holds potting soil, has a hole in the bottom, and does not fall over when the plant gets too big
- Potting soil
- Plant food
- Plants

What to DO:

❶ Fill the container with potting soil from a bag.

❷ Mix a little plant food into the potting soil.

❸ Loosen the roots of new plants before planting.

❹ Make spaces in the potting soil and put in the plants.

❺ Keep plants moist, but not wet all the time.

Try This

It is easier to have two or three different kinds of plants in one big pot, than a lot of little pots with one plant each. Plants in small pots need to be watered much more often, and they can outgrow their pots quickly.

Cool Stuff

Birds need water as much as they need food. Even butterflies and bees might come to your birdbath.

Teepee Birdbath

Make a place for birds to drink and take a bath that even the cat will have trouble climbing into!

What you NEED:
- Five or six long sticks (four or five feet long)
- Some wire or heavy twine
- Plastic dish or flowerpot saucer

What to DO:
1. Lay the sticks on the ground.
2. About a foot or two from one end, tie or wire them together really tightly.
3. Stand the teepee up, and spread the sticks out to form "legs."
4. Push the ends of the legs into the ground a little so that it is sturdy.
5. Put the plastic dish in the top and make sure it won't fall.
6. Fill with water whenever it gets dry.

Potato Bouquet

Flowers can be stuck into a potato—with a little help from you and some plastic straws!

What you NEED:
- Irish potato
- Kitchen knife
- Pencil
- Plastic drinking straws
- Flowers with long stems

What to DO:
❶ Cut a small slice on the bottom of the potato, so it won't roll around. (Be careful or get help using the knife!)

❷ Use the pencil to stick holes about halfway through the potato.

❸ Stick straws in the holes.

❹ Fill the straws with water.

❺ Put flowers in the straws.

Cool Stuff

People whose job it is to arrange flowers in vases are called "florists." They often put tall flowers in the middle, and shorter flowers on the sides so you can see them all better.

Compost

Everyone knows what happens to tree leaves in the forest. Worms and other creatures that live in the soil eat the leaves and turn them into good dirt. This is called composting, and you can do it in your own backyard. Then use the compost around your plants to help them grow better than ever.

What you NEED:
- A place to pile up stuff that won't be in the way
- Chicken wire, pieces of fencing, or wooden pallets (you can even paint them)
- Lots of leaves and grass clippings
- Kitchen scraps (not meat or cheese)—even eggshells, coffee grounds, and paper coffee pot filters

What to DO:
❶ Use three wooden pallets to make three sides of a compost box (leave the fourth side open so you can get to the compost).
❷ Pile leaves and grass clippings in the box, as high as you can.

Try This

You can make the composting process work faster if you keep the pile moist, and every week or so dig into it to help air and water move down into the pile.

❸ Mix in vegetable scraps, fruit peels, eggshells, and coffee grounds—make a little hole in the compost pile to put them in, and cover them up.

❹ When the weather is very dry, water the pile so the worms and other creatures can keep working.

❺ Dig into the bottom of the pile to find good compost that is ready to use.

Wildlife Garden

Plants and people are not the only living things in the garden—there are birds, butterflies, bees, frogs, toads, lizards, spiders, ants, snails, squirrels, roly-poly bugs, and many, many other kinds of wildlife out there. Most are good, but some can cause trouble if you get in their way.

What you NEED:

- Places for wildlife to nest and hide
- Food for them to eat
- Water

What to DO:

❶ Pile some leaves and woody branches in an out-of-the-way place, where bugs and other critters can hide during the day. Look in it from time to time to see what's there.

❷ Put out bird feeders and keep them filled all the time.

❸ Make a water garden or birdbath and keep water in it.

❹ Plant lots of different kinds of flowers, to attract different types of butterflies, and even hummingbirds.

❺ Raise a caterpillar in a big jar with holes in the top for air. Feed it leaves from whatever plant you found it on, and it may turn into a chrysalis (like a cocoon) and then into a butterfly. Then let it go.

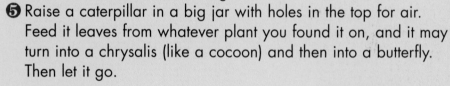

Cool Stuff

Always be very careful around flowers that attract butterflies, because bees love the same plants. And never kill a creature just for the fun of it, or because you are afraid—a good garden has a lot of different creatures, even the scary kinds.

Grass Creatures

Make funny creatures with old socks, pantyhose, and grass seed. A long sock can be a fuzzy worm. A short sock can be a head with grassy hair.

What you NEED:

- An old sock, or cut-off pantyhose legs
- Potting soil
- Plastic eyes
- Colored cotton balls
- Pipe cleaners
- Glue gun
- Grass seed

What to DO:

❶ Mix grass seed with potting soil.
❷ Stuff a sock or short piece of pantyhose with the seed-and-soil mix, and tie the end tightly.
❸ Put eyes and other face parts on with the glue gun. (Be careful—it's hot!)
❹ Put the worm on a plastic plate, or the head in a plastic cup.
❺ Water and the seeds will sprout and grow.
❻ Cut the "hair" with scissors when it gets too long. You may need to add plant food to the water every few weeks to keep it growing.

Cool Stuff

Rainbows may not always have a "pot of gold" at the end, but they always have the same colors, and in the same order: red, orange, yellow, green, blue, indigo, and violet. You can remember this by making the first letters of each color into the name ROY G. BIV.

Plant a Rainbow

You can make a long-lasting rainbow using flowers, with its own "pot of gold" at the end!

What you NEED:
- Plants that are the colors of the rainbow
- Good dirt in a sunny flower bed
- A big flower pot
- Gold or yellow paint

What to DO:
❶ Plant long, curved lines of each of the rainbow-colored plants. Put the plants close enough so they will grow together.
❷ Paint the pot gold or yellow and plant it with yellow flowers.
❸ Put the planted pot at one end of the rainbow.

Weather Station

Who needs to watch the weather on TV? You can find out what is going on outdoors for yourself, with a few simple weather tools in the garden.

What you NEED:

- Outdoor thermometer
- Rain gauge
- Long plastic ribbons or tape
- Notebook

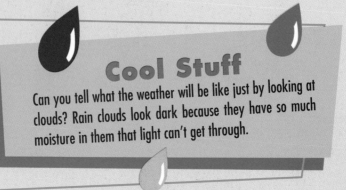

Cool Stuff

Can you tell what the weather will be like just by looking at clouds? Rain clouds look dark because they have so much moisture in them that light can't get through.

What to DO:

❶ Set the thermometer where it will not be in the sun (which warms it up too much).

❷ Put a rain gauge out in the open, where it will not be under a tree.

❸ Keep a record of temperatures and rainfall, and see if they are different from what the weather person on TV says.

❹ Tie the plastic ribbons together at one end, and hang this where the wind can blow them.

Fence Cup Design

Write something nice or make a design on a fence near your home, school, or church (but get permission from a grownup first).

What you NEED:

- Colorful plastic cups
- Chain link fence
- Pencil and paper

What to DO:

❶ Plan what you want to design, and see how many cups you will need of different colors.

❷ Stick the cups through the fence so they won't fall out or blow away.

❸ If any do blow away, be sure to pick them up so you don't leave a mess.

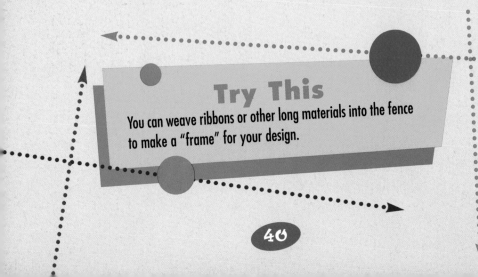

Try This

You can weave ribbons or other long materials into the fence to make a "frame" for your design.

Try This

Cut the tops off any root crop—a potato, carrot, or turnip will root and grow in a shallow container of water. So will some bulbs, such as paper-white narcissus and hyacinth.

Rooting Plants

Some plants grow roots even in plain water—and you can watch them grow! Two of the easiest plants to root are sweet potato vine and coleus.

What you NEED:
- Glass jar
- Rainwater
- Sunny window
- Plants to root

What to DO:
❶ Fill the jar with rainwater.
❷ Place it near (but not directly in) a sunny window.
❸ Cut stem sections of plants (six to eight inches long), and cut off the bottom few leaves. Stick them in the water.
❹ Keep the jar filled with water until roots begin to grow.
❺ When roots are big enough, put the plant in a pot of potting soil so it can grow bigger.

Art Garden

The garden is one of the most fun places to have art—even art you make yourself. It does not have to be fancy, or even very hard to make. The idea is to be creative and add things that will make you and your friends smile and laugh!

Here are just a few easy ideas that you can do—or come up with your own idea!

- Paint a rock.
- Make a scarecrow.
- Put shoes and boots on sticks.
- Put up a metal post and put magnets on it.
- Make concrete stepping stones, with marbles and other stuff in them.
- Paint a fence with hand-prints and butterflies.
- Make a worm by stringing together bottle caps.

- Paint a "labyrinth" on the lawn with spray paint.
- Make a bottle tree.
- Create a color garden using wooden posts painted different colors.
- Find different ways to make rainbows.
- Make an alphabet garden with plants for every letter (it will be hard to find an "X" plant!).
- Put toys among flowers and vegetables.
- Line a flower bed with old dishes or bottles.
- Paint leaves on a big board to use as a garden bench.
- Make a short poem about the plants you grow, or what you see or smell or touch in the garden.
- Paint a sign welcoming visitors to your garden.

Write with Plants

Say it with flowers—planted on a hillside or in a big pot. Good plants for writing words or letters are pansies, marigolds, dusty miller, Joseph's coat, or grass seed.

What you NEED:

- A big pot or sunny part of a flower bed
- Some pretty good soil or potting soil
- Lots of little plants
- Scissors or clippers

What to DO:

❶ Dig the dirt really well, and smooth it out.
❷ Set plants close together so they almost touch.
❸ Dig holes and plant.
❹ Water the plants to get them started.
❺ Use scissors to keep the plants neat.

Wattle Fence

Weave a fun fence like gardeners used to do a long time ago. "Over and under, in and out, that is what weaving is all about."

What you NEED:
- A lot of strong sticks (two or three feet long)
- Lots of twigs, vines, blades of tall grasses, stems of plants, and ribbons

What to DO:
❶ Push the sticks into the ground about six inches apart (this is easier to do when the ground is wet).
❷ Start near the bottom, and weave the twigs and other stuff in and out.

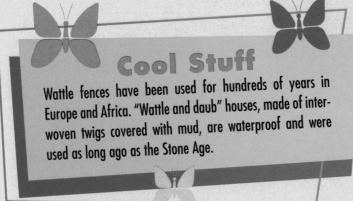

Cool Stuff

Wattle fences have been used for hundreds of years in Europe and Africa. "Wattle and daub" houses, made of interwoven twigs covered with mud, are waterproof and were used as long ago as the Stone Age.

Global Garden

Do you ever wonder where plants come from? You can grow flowers and vegetables from nearly every continent (except Antarctica) in your own backyard!

What you NEED:
- Any big ball or a big piece of plywood
- Waterproof marking pens
- Colored pens, paint, or spray paint

What to DO:
1. Look on the Internet or in a book for a map of the world.
2. Draw and color your own map on a big ball or flat piece of plywood.
3. Label the continents.
4. Look up different continents and countries to learn what plants grow there.

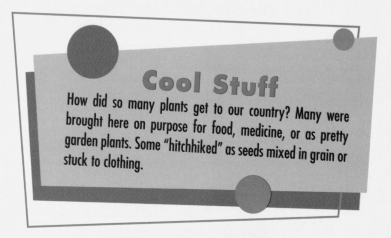

Cool Stuff

How did so many plants get to our country? Many were brought here on purpose for food, medicine, or as pretty garden plants. Some "hitchhiked" as seeds mixed in grain or stuck to clothing.

❺ Find some of these plants to grow in your own garden, and label where they come from:
- **Africa:** aloe, gladiolus, globe amaranth, periwinkle, pentas
- **South America:** coleus, sweet potato, cleome, elephant's ear, pepper
- **Asia:** daylily, caladium, rubber tree, lily
- **North America:** corn, potato, sunflower, beans, purple coneflower
- **Europe:** daffodil, lettuce, rosemary, artemisia
- **Australia:** eucalyptus, kangaroo paw, bottlebrush, mint bush

Tire Sculptures

Find a good way to use old tires, and have some fun, too! You can stack them to make a snowman or Christmas tree, or fill them with good dirt or potting soil and grow plants in them.

What you NEED:
- Old car tires
- Paint
- Decorations

What to DO:
❶ Stack the tires up so that they won't fall over.
❷ For a snowman, you can put bigger tires in the middle.

❸ For a Christmas tree, put smaller tires near the top.
❹ Paint them white or green.
❺ Add decorations.
❻ For a planter, paint the tire, fill it with potting soil, plant plants in it, water.

Dinosaur Puzzle

Create your own scary creature for the garden—but make a small one indoors first to practice. Try inventing a new kind of animal, or a dinosaur. It can have a lot of parts, or just a few.

What you NEED:

- Sheets of cardboard
- Drawing supplies
- Sharp scissors
- Plywood
- Saw
- Paint

What to DO:

1. Draw a crazy animal on paper.
2. Practice making a small one first. Draw a body, two sets of legs, and antlers, ears, or horns on cardboard.
3. Cut it out, and see how it all fits together.
4. Have a grownup make your crazy creature out of wood.
5. Paint it and put it outside.

Water Gardening

Every garden is better when it has a pond—even a very small one. You can make a simple water garden without a lot of help!

What you NEED:

- Anything that will hold water—a big bucket, a small wading pool, even a washtub or old bathtub
- Rocks, shells, driftwood
- Water garden plants
- And of course you need water!

Cool Stuff

Frogs and toads will lay eggs in your water garden in the spring, which hatch into tadpoles, then grow into adults. Tadpoles, frogs, and little fish eat mosquito larvae swimming in the water.

Try This

After a few weeks, look really closely at your pond garden and you'll see different types of small creatures in it, including insects. If you look at a sample of the water under a microscope you'll see even more!

What to DO:

❶ Put the container where it will get some sunshine, and fill it with water.

❷ Put pretty rocks, shells, or pieces of wood around the edges.

❸ Add one or two water garden plants if you can find them at a garden center.

❹ If you want to add fish, use cheap gold fish from a pet store, and feed them once a week with gold fish food (be careful—too much food can make fish sick).

Pot Man

Make a funny man to watch over your garden all day and all night!

What you NEED:

- Several cans or plastic pots of different sizes
- Plastic or metal funnel
- Ribbon or twine
- Hole puncher or hammer and nail

What to DO:

1. Lay out your pot man, with the larger pots for the body and head, and the smaller pots for the arms and legs. Use the funnel as a hat.
2. Punch holes where you need them to tie all the pots together.
3. Use ribbon or twine to tie the pots together.
4. Paint the pot man.

Try This

You can also make a garden person out of plastic plates tied together with ribbons pulled through punched holes.

Try This

You can also put bottles on the ends of short, sturdy branches to make a bottle tree. Use different kinds of bottles for a colorful display—blue, brown, green, and clear.

CD Tree

Scare birds and bring flashy fun into your garden—with throw-away stuff.

What you NEED:

- A big branch from a tree, or a small tree or shrub
- Old CDs
- String or ribbon

What to DO:

❶ Dig a hole.
❷ Stand the branch or tree up in the hole, or tie it to a fence post.
❸ Hang CDs from the branches with string.

Raised Beds

When Captain John Smith first sailed to America, his settlers found that their vegetable and herb gardens stayed too wet during part of the year. So they made gardens that were on top of the ground. A small raised garden can be planted earlier in the spring, with more plants close together, and watered only when the weather is dry.

What you NEED:
- Good dirt in a sunny part of the yard
- Bags of potting soil
- Shovel and rake
- Three long boards (all the same length)
- Saw
- Nails
- Plants
- Mulch

What to DO:

❶ Cut one board in half, so you have two long and two short boards.

❷ Nail the boards together to make a rectangle.

❸ Dig the dirt inside the rectangle as deeply as you can.

❹ Spread the potting soil over the top.

❺ Mix the dirt and potting soil together really well.

❻ Plant flowers, vegetables, herbs, and bulbs in the raised bed.

❼ Spread mulch over the top of the soil, to help the garden grow better.

Try This

Raised beds are easy to grow plants in, and you can have something growing in them nearly all the time. Plant a variety of vegetables—some like hot weather and some like it cool— or different kinds of flowers that bloom at different times.

Dried Fruit Slices

Birds and kids love dried fruit slices, but fresh fruit turns brown and can go bad quickly. Cooking takes a little more work than other projects, but with a little help from a grownup you can make dried fruit slices that will last a long time.

What you NEED:

- Fresh fruit (apples, oranges, bananas, lemons)
- Sharp knife
- Lemon juice
- Small bowl
- Baking sheet
- Oven

Cool Stuff

Find as many different fruits and vegetables as you can at the grocery store—in a rainbow of colors. Can you eat a rainbow every day?

Try This

You can also pick leaves from mint and basil plants, wash them really well, put them in ice cube trays, fill with water, and freeze to use in the winter.

What to DO:

❶ With help from a grownup, carefully cut the fruit into thin slices, a few pieces at a time.

❷ As each piece gets cut, dip it in lemon juice— this keeps it from turning brown.

❸ Spread the slices on a cookie sheet.

❹ Bake for an hour in an oven turned on "low"— not too hot—until the slices are dry.

❺ Keep the unused fruit slices in a sealed container in the refrigerator until you are ready to use them.

Vine Teepee

Make a place to sit quietly and read or talk that is private but pretty. To make a teepee big enough to get inside, use poles eight or ten feet long and weave string between all but two poles (to leave a door!).

What you NEED:

- Four or five long sticks or metal poles (eight or ten feet long)
- Strong string or wire
- Plants or seeds of vines

What to DO:

❶ Lay the sticks or poles down, and tie them together near one end with string or wire.

❷ Stand the teepee up and spread the bottoms of the poles apart.

❸ Push the ends into the ground to make it sturdy.

❹ Plant vines, from plants or seeds, by each pole.

❺ Water the plants when they get dry.

Try This

Some vines wrap around things on their own, but others have to be tied gently with soft string or ribbons.

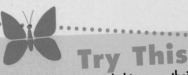

Try This

If you tie a plastic mesh bag full of dryer lint, string, and hair from a hairbrush outside where birds can find it, they will use the stuff for making nests.

Feed the Birds

Help our feathered friends find something good to eat.

What you NEED:

- Orange halves
- Pine cones
- Knife
- Heavy string
- Birdseed
- Peanut butter
- Shortening

What to DO:

1. Clean the pulp out of the orange halves.
2. Carefully cut holes in the sides near the top.
3. Pull pieces of string through the holes and tie the ends together.
4. Fill with birdseed and hang outside where birds can find it.
5. Tie a string around a pine cone.
6. Mash a mixture of peanut butter and shortening into it.
7. Roll it in birdseed before hanging it from a tree limb.

Easy Scarecrow

Scarecrows have been made for many hundreds of years. Creating a scarecrow of your own can make your garden more fun—even if you don't want to keep birds away! There are many ways to make one, but here is the easiest.

What you NEED:

- Broomstick or other skinny pole
- Plastic milk jug, plate, gourd
- Coat hanger
- Tape
- Long-sleeved shirt or dress
- Hat
- Marking pens

What to DO:

❶ Straighten out the top of the coat hanger, and tape it near the top of the broomstick.

❷ Put the long-sleeved shirt or dress on the hanger— no need for legs or pants!

❸ Make a face on the milk jug and put the jug on top of the scarecrow.

❹ Stand the scarecrow in your garden.

❺ Try making arms out of cut-off branches from a tree, stuck in the sleeves.

Try This

You can also stuff some old clothes with plastic bags and make a head out of a bucket or plastic plate. You can even make a whole family of scarecrows!

Grow Some Mold

Mold growing on things is part of the natural process of decay. Grow an icky but interesting "miniature world" of mold on bread or an orange peel and look at the beautiful patterns.

What you NEED:
- Glass jar with tight-fitting lid
- Piece of bread or an orange peel
- A little water
- Magnifying lens

What to DO:
❶ Wipe a windowsill or part of the floor with the piece of bread or orange peel.
❷ Put just a few drops of water on one corner of the bread or peel, to make it barely moist.
❸ Put the bread or peel in the jar, and screw on the lid.
❹ Put the jar in a warm place in the kitchen away from sunlight.
❺ Use a magnifying glass to look closely at the mold that grows.

Try This
Different molds grow in dry and moist places, in dark places and bright light. Try putting pieces of bread or orange peel in different areas and see what happens.

Cool Stuff

A maze is a puzzle that has turns and dead ends. A labyrinth is a curving path leading to a destination (see photo on page 11).

Daffodil Maze

Plant flowers around a long, winding walkway—it will make you slow down and enjoy them!

What you NEED:
- Pencil and paper
- Spray paint
- A big bag of bulbs
- Small flowering plants

What to DO:
❶ Practice drawing a maze or labyrinth on paper.
❷ Draw it on the grass with spray paint—make sure the paths between the lines are three feet wide to give room to run!
❸ Dig a trench where the paint is.
❹ Plant the bulbs and other flowers in the trench.

Indoor Worm Box

You would be surprised to learn how many people grow worms indoors—to eat their garbage and turn it into good soil! It is easy, and does not have to be messy or smelly.

What you NEED:

- Plastic sweater box with a tight fitting lid
- Shredded newspaper
- Chopped vegetable scraps, fruit peels, eggshells
- Box of "red wriggler" fishing worms

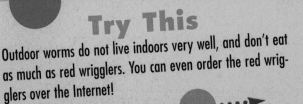

Try This

Outdoor worms do not live indoors very well, and don't eat as much as red wrigglers. You can even order the red wrigglers over the Internet!

What to DO:

❶ Cut or tear newspaper into long, thin strips (tear from the top of the page downward), enough to almost fill the box.

❷ Moisten it with just a little water—make it moist, but not soggy wet.

❸ Stir in some finely chopped vegetable scraps, banana peels, and eggshells.

❹ Add the worms and keep the box closed tight to keep the worms inside.

❺ Every few days add a little more dry newspaper strips, to keep it from being too wet.

❻ "Harvest" the worm compost by feeding the worms scraps one night, and scooping out the bottom layer of compost the next morning.

❼ Use the compost as fertilizer for potted plants.

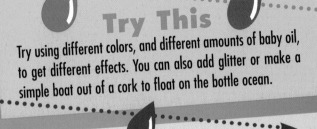

Try This

Try using different colors, and different amounts of baby oil, to get different effects. You can also add glitter or make a simple boat out of a cork to float on the bottle ocean.

Ocean in a Bottle

Create the same slow-motion rolling that the ocean has, in a hand-held bottle.

What you NEED:

- Mixing bowl and funnel
- Clear plastic cola bottle with cap
- One pint of water
- One pint of baby oil or vegetable oil
- Two or three drops of blue food coloring

What to DO:

❶ Mix the water, baby oil or vegetable oil, and food coloring in the bowl.
❷ Pour carefully into the clear plastic bottle using the funnel.
❸ Gently tap to get all the air bubbles out.
❹ Put the cap on very tightly.
❺ Turn the bottle on its side and tilt it back and forth.

Easy Plants

WILD PLANTS grow by themselves, if their seeds sprout in good soil, and sunshine and rain help young plants grow. Many more kinds of plants can be grown in a small garden, where YOU do some of the things that nature does for wild plants.

Plants NEED soil, sunshine, water, and plant food or fertilizer. And they need YOU to put them in the right place, and TAKE CARE of them.

Sooner or later, everyone wants to grow flowers and other kinds of plants.

All SORTS of plants can be grown, and they can be mixed together—tall ones, short ones, some with flowers, others with pretty leaves, or even parts you can eat!

Some plants are easier than others. This chapter has a lot of the very easiest, most FUN types of plants to grow—even some that grow really well in pots. All you need to do to get them started is DIG a place in the dirt, ADD stuff to it, and either spread seeds over the ground or set plants into holes. After that they will need watering and feeding. Give a few of these plants a try, and see how much fun you can have!

Tools You Will Need:

Gloves

Shovel

Hand trowel (little hand-sized shovel)

Garden rake

Pencil and paper

Garden hose

Watering can

Bucket

Potting soil or compost

Pots

What kind of soil do plants need?

Plant ROOTS grow down into the soil, where they can get water, nutrients, and oxygen, and so they are anchored firmly and won't fall over. Most garden soil gets dry and becomes really hard in the sun. Add stuff to it to help make it fluffy, so that plant roots will have AIR, and so the soil will absorb WATER. Gardeners add compost, old leaves, or potting soil from a bag. It does not take very much—most gardeners spread a layer about two inches deep, then stir it into the soil as far as a shovel can go. Mix it in really well.

How much light do plants need?

Plants need SUNLIGHT for photosynthesis. The green parts of plants absorb the sunlight and turn it into energy the plant uses to grow. Some plants need sun all day, or at least half a day. Others need bright light, such as under a tall tree. And others need a SHADY place, like in the shadow of the house. Plants can get sunlight even in the shade, but most plants won't be happy in a really dark place.

How often should you water?

Plant ROOTS take up water and it is sent upward into the rest of the plant. A plant that is thirsty will droop, but you can revive it by watering right away. If a plant goes without water for too long it can die. Some plants need A LOT of water (some even grow in ponds or streams) but others need VERY LITTLE (like desert plants). Potted plants outside on your porch or deck need water more often than plants in the ground, but potted plants indoors don't need to be watered very often.

If you are growing plants from SEEDS, sprinkle a little water over them every day or two until they sprout, then give them a little extra water every few days until they start growing well. If you set out SMALL PLANTS, water them right after you plant them and water again every other day until they get set-tled. After plants in the ground are growing well, water once every week or once every other week, depending on how much rain your garden gets. It is IMPORTANT to not keep them too wet, or let them stay dry for too long.

How do you feed plants?

Plants get a lot of their nutrition from the soil and air, but some types of plants need EXTRA food. There are TWO kinds of plant food—the dry kind that you sprinkle over the top of the soil, and the kind you mix with water and pour around plant roots. Dry plant food lasts in the soil for a long time, but the wet kind needs to be put on plants every few weeks. Always use EXACTLY the amount the directions tell you to—if you use too much it will hurt the plants!

How do you plant plants?

Plants can be grown from SEEDS or you can buy SMALL PLANTS from a garden center or nursery. Sometimes a friend or relative or neighbor might even share seeds or plants from their own garden. After digging your garden soil to loosen it up, sprinkle seeds—not TOO close together, or the plants won't have room to grow. Push BIG seeds a little further into the soil (but not too deep!). If you are planting small plants, loosen their roots to help them grow out into the soil better, and put them just deep enough to cover their roots with dirt. Press the soil firmly around their roots. WATER new plants and seeds to settle the soil and get them started. You can also spread a thin layer of mulch to keep roots cool, and to keep the soil from drying out.

Awesome Annuals

Annuals are plants that have to be planted every year from seed or from little plants. Most of them have pretty FLOWERS, but others have interesting LEAVES. Most annuals make lots of seeds you can save to plant the next year, or share with your friends.

There are two main kinds of annuals—those that grow best in the HOT summer, and those that like COOL weather and can be grown in the fall or very late winter and early spring. Some annuals are easy to grow in pots. Annuals grow so fast you need to TAKE CARE of them by fixing the soil before you plant, watering them when they get dry, and giving them plant food, too.

Annuals need:

- Good soil to grow deep roots
- Sun or bright light
- Water when they get dry
- Feeding every few weeks with plant food

Here are a few EASY annuals you can grow. Have fun putting different colors, sizes, and textures together.

Black-Eyed Susan
(sun)

There are several kinds of this fun wildflower. Each of its flowers is really a group of many tiny blooms. The thin yellow, gold, or red flowers are called "ray" flowers, and the brown or green "nose cone" is made of "disk" flowers. Butterflies really love this plant.

Celosia
(sun)

The two main kinds of celosia are "cockscomb," which looks like the top of a rooster's head, and "prince's feather," which looks like a tall feather. They both love hot weather and sometimes drop many seeds on the ground to grow into plants the next year.

Cleome
(sun or part shade)

This plant is sometimes called "cat's whiskers" or even "spider flower" because the long, thin seedpods stand straight out. The leaves are a little sticky and it has a few small thorns. The seeds are easy to save. This plant stands up above other summer flowers.

Coleus
(sun or part shade)

These big plants have very colorful leaves and spikes of pretty little flowers that butterflies like. Some grow well in lots of sun, but many do very well in shady flower beds or pots. The stems root very easily in water to make new plants. This plant is in the mint family— notice how square its stems are.

Cosmos
(sun or part shade)
The skinny seeds of cosmos sprout very quickly in sunny weather, and the flowers grow all summer—and are covered with butterflies! This plant can be grown with other annuals for a wildflower look. Seeds are very easy to save.

Dusty Miller
(sun, part shade, shade)
Grow this little plant for its beautiful white or gray leaves that make it really stand out in the garden. It loves to be in the front of a flower garden, or in a big pot where it looks great by itself or with other plants. Don't water it too much!

Globe Amaranth
(sun)

Lots of bristly, round flowers, each about the size of a thimble, grow on long stems all summer and attract butterflies. The flowers are easy to cut, tie together in bunches, and hang upside down indoors to dry for making flower arrangements.

Johnny Jump-Ups
(sun)

The little flowers are usually yellow and purple with "cat whisker" stripes. They flower best in cool weather—gardeners in southern regions plant them in the fall and enjoy them all winter. Grow them in flower beds or pots, and mixed with bulbs.

Marigold
(sun or part shade)
There are many different kinds of marigolds. There are little plants that look good in pots or near the front of a flower bed, and tall kinds that butterflies love. They make great bouquet flowers. Most have yellow or orange flowers and the plants have a funny scent.

Moss Rose
(sun)
Short moss rose plants have fat little leaves and lots of bright flowers that open when the sun is shining and close when the sun goes down or on a cloudy day. They grow best in the front of a hot, sunny flower bed or in a pot. They drop seeds that sprout into new plants the next year.

Nasturtium

(sun or part shade)

The big, almost completely round leaves of this fast-growing plant show off the bright yellow or orange flowers— that some people like to eat! The plant grows best in cool weather, and is hard to grow in the southern parts of the country where nights stay hot.

Pansy

(sun or part shade)

Set little plants in pots or in flower beds with bulbs, for cool-season flowers with happy "faces" in all the colors of the rainbow. In fact, you can plant an entire "rainbow garden" with just pansies! The flowers can be eaten in salads.

Pentas
(sun or part shade)

This plant comes from Egypt, and has big clusters of little star-like flowers all summer and fall. It is also called Egyptian star flower. This is one of the very best flowers for bringing butterflies and hummingbirds into your garden. It grows best in hot weather.

Periwinkle
(sun)

Cheerful little periwinkle plants are covered in even the hottest times of summer with pin-wheels of white, red, or pink flowers. They do not like to be wet, so plant them where they get lots of sun, or in pots where they can get a little dry between waterings.

Petunia
(sun or part shade)
This old-fashioned, fast-growing flower can really spread out, so give it room to grow! Its very wide, trumpet-shaped flowers are fun for hummingbirds and butterflies, and they have a spicy scent that reminds older gardeners of their mothers' and grandmothers' gardens.

Snapdragon
(sun or part shade)
Snapdragons can be tall or short, with flower spikes of white, yellow, pink, and other colors. The tall ones are great to grow behind shorter plants. If you are very careful, you can gently pinch a flower to make it open like a dragon's mouth. Snapdragons grow best in cool weather, or over the winter in southern regions.

Sunflower
(sun)

Sunflowers are one of the easiest plants to grow from seed. Plant them when the soil warms up in late spring, in rows or in small groups— don't crowd them since they need room to grow. Some varieties are tall, some short, and the seeds of some are great for birds and kids to eat!

Zinnia
(sun)

There are many kinds of zinnias, from small low-growing ones to tall kinds that make great butterfly and bouquet flowers. Sow seeds when the soil warms up in the spring, and the plants will grow and bloom all summer. Cut off faded flowers to make plants bloom even more.

Very Good Veggies

Most vegetables are ANNUALS and have to be planted every year. They can be grown just like other annuals. Farmers use tractors and other farm tools to grow vegetables in long rows, but you can plant them ANYWHERE or any way you like—in rows, in raised beds, in big pots or buckets. Some are pretty enough to grow even in flower gardens!

Vegetables grow FAST, so you have to help take care of them by making the soil good before you plant, and watering them when they get dry. Most vegetables are EASY to find in garden stores as seeds or small plants.

Each type of vegetable has MANY different kinds, shapes, colors, and even flavors, so be sure to look at pictures on seed packets before deciding which kinds of each you will grow in your own garden.

Some vegetables grow best in the HOT summer: corn, cucumber, eggplant, okra, pepper, pumpkin, beans, and tomato. Some vegetables like COOL weather and can be grown in the late winter or late summer: lettuce, carrot, radish, potato, and sugar snap peas.

Vegetables need:

- Pretty good soil
- Sun
- Water when they get dry
- Feeding every few weeks with plant food
- Regular harvesting (picking), so they will keep making more vegetables

Here are a few vegetables that you can grow. Who knows, you might even EAT some!

Carrot
(sun)

Carrots grow in the cool part of the year. There are many different kinds—some are long and thin like fingers, some are short and stubby like a fat thumb. The leaves look like ferns. Carrots can even grow in pots if you keep them in the sun and water them a lot.

Corn
(sun)

Corn is a tall, skinny plant with long leaves. It can be grown in long rows, or mixed with other plants—just be sure you can get to the ears to eat them! There are many kinds, including popcorn, strawberry corn, Indian corn, and sweet corn.

Cucumber
(sun)

Grow cucumbers in the summer when the weather is warm. Their stems are very long and will trail on the ground, but you can train them up a fence or on an easy trellis made from sticks and wire. You can eat cucumbers right out of the garden, but wash and peel them first!

Eggplant
(sun)

You will love the big leaves and purple flowers of eggplant, and the big shiny purple or green fruits! Some kinds are even white and the same size as eggs, or long and skinny. Eggplants are heavy and can make the plant fall over if you don't tie it to a sturdy stick.

Lettuce
(sun or part shade)

Salads are made mostly with lettuce, but there are a lot of different kinds—more than you see at a restaurant. It can have straight or curly leaves and comes in many colors, even red. Lettuce likes cool weather and is easy to grow in pots, even on a porch.

Okra
(sun)

This tall plant with big leaves is grown for food in the south-ern part of the country and is related to cotton and hibiscus plants. It has big, pretty, light yellow flowers and long, pointed seedpods that can be cooked when they are still small and soft. Stems with seedpods can also be dried and used like dried flowers.

Peas
(sun)

These vines have pretty white flowers. The peas are the seeds of the plant. Before the peas begin to grow inside the pods, the little pods can be eaten raw right off the vine (they are very sweet!) or cooked. Sugar snap peas grow best in cool weather, or planted in the late winter in warmer regions.

Pepper
(sun)

There are many kinds of peppers. Sweet peppers are used in a lot of foods, and are very rich in vitamins. Hot peppers are used in many foods from other countries, like Mexico, to make foods spicy. The little peppers grown in flower beds with pretty colors like red, yellow, or even purple, are very, very hot—if you touch them, wash your hands before wiping your eyes or they will burn!

Potato
(sun)

Get a grownup to help cut potatoes into pieces (each with a little "eye") and plant as soon as you can dig in the garden in the late winter. New potatoes grow on the stems in the dark, so as the plants grow, cover the stems with dirt or leaves. They can even be grown in tire planters.

Pumpkin
(sun)

These summer vines need LOTS of room to grow— even the "baby pumpkin" varieties. They need hot dirt to thrive, so wait until the ground has warmed in the spring. Plant the big seeds in small hills made in the soil. Water often all summer for big pumpkins in the fall.

Radish
(sun)

Very few kids eat radishes, but they are so easy to grow, and so fast, you should give them a try. Sow the seeds very thinly over the ground and sprinkle with water every day or two. Different kinds of radishes have different shapes—some are very round and some are long and thin.

Sweet Potato
(sun or part shade)

This fast-growing, ground-hugging vine has thick roots shaped a lot like a regular potato that can be baked and eaten. Sweet potatoes are very high in vitamins. They need very little water or fertilizer to spread across a big area. Pieces of the vine can form roots if placed in a glass of water.

Swiss Chard
(sun or part shade)
The colorful stems of this plant can be green, red, yellow, or even orange. The leaves can be broken or cut off and cooked exactly like spinach. It grows well in flower gardens as well as vegetable gardens.

Tomato
(sun)
There are lots of different kinds of tomatoes, including sweet little "cherry" tomatoes and big ones that can be sliced for sandwiches. Tomatoes are vines that need really good dirt, regular watering and feeding, and something to grow on like a fence or tomato cage. Eat them right off the vine (but wash them first).

Terrific Herbs

Herbs are the most USEFUL kinds of plants! You can say the word "herb" either *with* or *without* the "H" sound— either way is okay. They are plants whose plant parts (mostly leaves) we use for flavoring FOOD or making tea, soap, medicine, or nice-smelling perfume. Some are just FUN to have around because they have a lot of history. A few are also very good butterfly plants.

Some gardeners grow herbs in a special HERB GARDEN, but others just grow them like regular annuals or perennials, in big pots, raised beds, flower beds, or vegetable gardens. Most herbs are best bought as little plants from a garden center. There are many DIFFERENT kinds of each type of herb, so don't be afraid to rub a leaf to smell it, and make sure you get what you like the best.

Herbs need:

- Pretty good soil that does not stay wet
- At least a few hours of sunshine
- Regular watering, but don't let them stay dry or wet
- A little plant food every few weeks

Here are a few VERY easy herbs to try. Once you get them growing well, add MORE, and try different kinds. The next time you eat pizza or spaghetti, remember, you're EATING herbs!

Anise Hyssop
(sun or part shade)
The leaves on this plant smell like licorice and can be used to make a nice tea. Its lilac or blue flowers are on tall stems that make the plant very good for growing behind shorter flowers. It is very attractive to butterflies and bees.

Basil
(sun or part shade)
Grow this plant mostly for the leaves, which smell really good after a rain or when you touch them. Use the leaves to give flavor to soups, sandwiches, spaghetti, or anything that has tomatoes in it. There are lots of different kinds, even some with dark purple or frilly leaves.

Chives

(sun or part shade)

When cut, the skinny leaves of this herb smell just like onions (chives, onions, and garlic are all in the same plant family), and they can be used for cooking. The summer flowers are spiny balls of light purple (which can be eaten also).

Fennel

(sun)

This is a very tall plant, with soft, feathery leaves. It smells just like licorice. You may see swallowtail butterfly caterpillars on it in the summer because it's one of their favorite foods. Let the caterpillars eat all they want so they will turn into beautiful butterflies. The fennel will recover and make new leaves.

Lavender
(sun or part shade)

The small flowers of lavender have been used in perfumes for many centuries. The name of the color lavender comes from this plant, since it has pale purple flowers. The leaves are also fragrant.

Mint
(sun or part shade)

There are many different kinds of mint, including spearmint, orange mint, chocolate mint, and apple mint. They love moist soils, so water them often—or plant by a downspout or air conditioner that drips a lot! These plants spread quickly by underground stems.

Oregano

(sun or part shade)

This spreading plant is where the spice oregano comes from for flavoring spaghetti, chili, pizza, and lots of other foods. It has pretty purplish flowers in the summer, and grows well along the edge of a flower bed or in an herb garden.

Parsley

(sun or part shade)

Parsley is used in a lot of foods, and sometimes a sprig of it is put on the plate just to look pretty. It can have flat or curly leaves, but the flat type is best for cook- ing. Swallowtail butterfly caterpillars like to eat pars- ley and some people plant it just for them.

Rosemary
(sun or part shade)

This very easy herb has long stems with skinny leaves that smell very good and are used for cooking. For a special treat, the little blue flowers can be eaten! Rosemary comes from dry, rocky places near the Mediterranean Sea and its strong scent and rough texture keep animals from eating it.

Thyme
(sun)

Some herbs are just fun to grow. There are many different kinds of thyme (pronounced "time"), but most grow very low and spread out, making them great along the front of a garden, in pots, or in a rock garden. Brush your hand across a patch of thyme to release the fragrance from the leaves and flowers into the air.

Wonderful Vines

Vines are plants with long, skinny STEMS that cannot stand up on their own, and have to CLIMB on trees, fences, or other tall things. They are interesting to grow, but they ALSO have great looking leaves and sometimes beautiful flowers and even fruit to eat.

Vines use DIFFERENT ways to climb. Some just WRAP their stems around whatever they're growing on, and you may need to help them get started. Others have little ROOTS on their stems that grow onto the bark of trees, or the sides of walls, fences, or houses. Some even have little parts called "TENDRILS" that reach out like little arms to grab and wrap around things. And some wrap the stalks of their leaves on their supports.

Vines need:

- Sun or part sun
- Pretty good dirt
- Something nearby they can climb on
- Help getting started climbing
- Watering when they get dry
- Feeding every few weeks

Here are just a few easy vines you can grow. Plant them so they can grow on different types of STRUCTURES, like teepees, trellises, or fences.

Black-Eyed Susan Vine

(sun or part shade)

This fast-growing little vine has beautiful yellow flowers all summer. Each flower has a dark "eye" that gives the plant its name. Grow it on some sticks tied into a "teepee" shape, or on a fence where it can get lots of sun.

Cypress Vine

(sun)

This little vine grows so fast it can cover a fence or even tall plants growing nearby! The leaves look like ferns (or the leaves of a cypress tree), and the little, bright red flowers are loved by butterflies and hummingbirds. Seeds drop on the ground and sprout the next year.

Gourds
(sun)

Many different kinds of gourds—even some for making birdhouses—have been grown around the world for a very long time. Plant the big seeds in the spring beside a fence so the vines can grow up while the gourds hang down. The big summer flowers turn into fun gourds in the fall. Loofah gourds can be soaked in water and "peeled" like an orange, and the insides used as a foot or back scrubber in the bathtub.

Hyacinth Bean
(sun or part shade)

This big vine grows quickly and is covered with very dark green leaves, spikes of pink flowers, and fat reddish-purple beans. Because it grows so fast, this vine is great for making a hidden garden.

Moonflower
(sun or part shade)
This big vine needs a fence or something else to grow on. The large white flowers have a very sweet scent, and twist open late in the afternoon—just as it's getting dark—to attract big night-flying moths. The seeds are slow to sprout, so soak them overnight in a glass of water to help get them started.

Morning Glory
(sun)
This old-fashioned vine has been a favorite flower for many years. It has big flowers of white, pink, red, blue, or purple that open only in the morning and close when the sun gets hot. It grows best on a fence or homemade trellis, and the seeds are easy to save.

Scarlet Runner Bean
(sun)

This vine has been popular for a long time. It has light green leaves and blooms with bright red-orange flowers before forming beans. Grow it in the summer on "teepees" made out of sticks tied at the top, on a fence, or around a hidden garden.

Sweet Pea
(sun)

There are many kinds of this vine, which has very sweet-smelling flowers. The seeds are slow to sprout, so soak them overnight in water. The plants will grow on a fence or trellis. They grow best in cool weather. In warmer regions, plant the seeds in late winter.

Pretty Perennials

Perennials are plants that grow for MANY years. Most have beautiful FLOWERS, but some are grown just for their pretty LEAVES. Most perennials "die down" for part of the year, but sprout new leaves and flowers the next year from their roots and stems. Some also drop SEEDS to start new plants. Some perennials are easy to grow in pots, but most do best when they are planted in good flower bed dirt.

Perennials need:

- Good soil to grow deep roots
- The right amount of sun or shade
- Water when they get very dry
- Feeding at least once a year with plant food
- Tall kinds may fall over and need to be tied to a stick (called "staking")

Perennial plants grow in the same spot for many years, so start them out right by fixing the soil. There are good perennials for SUNNY gardens, and others for very SHADY gardens. Some will grow in either kind of garden. Most perennials will grow a long time without extra water. Be prepared to water them once every two or three weeks, or more often if the weather is hot, dry, and windy. But do not keep perennials wet or they may die.

Some perennials grow easily from seeds. Most take a long time to get big enough to flower, so gardeners just set out little plants. After digging a hole in the dirt, CAREFULLY loosen roots of perennials, spread the roots out in the hole, and cover them with soil. Do not plant perennials too deeply or their stems or crowns may rot. Most perennial plants grow in bunches that can be dug up, pulled or cut apart, and replanted. This is an easy way to create and SHARE new plants.

Artemisia
(sun or part shade)
This plant has light gray leaves like the annual called "dusty miller" but it is more like a shrub. It can be cut and dried for making wreaths. The leaves smell funny, and can repel insects.

Balloon Flower
(sun)
The stems of this plant have lots of blue, purple, pink, or white flowers that look like balloons until they open up into fat stars. When it dies down in the winter, it takes a long time to come back up the next spring—so don't dig it up by accident!

Bee Balm
(sun or part shade)
The leaves of bee balm—which is also called by its Latin name "monarda"—are very fragrant and can be made into tea. Red or pink flowers are very attractive to hummingbirds and butterflies, and taste spicy when eaten.

Canna
(sun)
Big roots sprout tall stems of huge, colorful leaves topped by very interesting flowers. On the west coast and southern areas of the country cannas can be left in the ground over the winter, but in the north they have to be dug up and replanted the next spring.

Daisy
(sun)

Daisies are great for butterflies and bouquets. They are usually white with a yellow center, and flower in spring and summer. You can make a necklace of daisies—cut several daisies (with stems), pierce the stem of one and pull another stem through the hole, and so on until they are linked together. This is called a daisy chain.

Dandelion
(sun or part shade)

These beautiful yellow flowers and fuzzy seedheads upset some grownups when they grow in the lawn. But they really do not hurt anything, are pretty, and are great for bees and butterflies, so why not enjoy them as wildflowers? You can eat them, too!

109

Daylily
(sun or part shade)

There are many different daylilies, all very easy to grow. The common orange one is easy to divide to plant in your own garden. Small kinds, with names like 'Stella d'Oro', flower again and again all summer. It is called daylily because each flower is only open for one day. All daylily flower buds can be eaten!

Fern
(shade, some sun)

When the little "fiddleheads" of ferns start coming up and uncurling, you know it's spring! Ferns were growing when dinosaurs were alive. They have very interesting leaves (called "fronds") and grow very well in shady or even wet gardens. Ferns don't have flowers or seeds. They grow from dust-like "spores," which come from the brown dots on the backs of the fern leaves.

Goldenrod
(sun)

This wildflower is very popular as a fall-blooming bouquet flower. Some grownups don't plant it in gardens because it is common and is found growing wild in fields. But butterflies love it, and it does not cause sneezing!

Hollyhock
(sun or part shade)

One of the tallest flowers for a garden, hollyhock has big round leaves and tall spikes of big flowers that butterflies love. The seeds are very easy to collect and plant in other places. Plant hollyhock in the back of a flower bed, where it will not hide other flowers.

Hosta
(shade)

This is one of the easiest perennials of all to divide, plant, and grow! The leaves are big and can be green, nearly yellow, blue, or even striped. Sometimes slugs and snails eat holes in the leaves, but it keeps growing new leaves!

Iris
(sun or shade)

Iris gets its name from the ancient rainbow goddess because its flowers come in all the colors of the rainbow. It blooms mostly in the spring, but the sword-like leaves, which look great all summer, make iris a perfect perennial to plant with other flowers.

Lamb's Ears
(sun or part shade)

Fuzzy gray-white leaves make this a favorite plant for petting! Lamb's ears look best when they are grown in front of other plants, to help show off colorful flowers. It must be planted in good dirt that doesn't stay wet, or its stems can rot.

Ornamental Grasses
(sun)

There are many good grasses that grow into big clumps with green or even striped leaves. The interesting summer and fall clusters of small flowers look like plumes or fox tails. Old leaves turn light brown in the winter, and can be spray-painted to make them pretty before cutting them down in early spring.

Phlox
(sun or part shade)
There are many different kinds of phlox (pronounced "flocks"), which are all wildflowers and attract butterflies and hummingbirds. Some bloom in the spring with blue, white, or pink flowers, some are tall and have pink, white, or red flowers. Phlox flowers have a very sweet scent.

Purple Coneflower
(sun or part shade)
This wildflower has long stems topped with big, orange, bristly "cones" surrounded by long, pink, purple, or white daisy-like flower petals. Butterflies really love purple coneflowers since the flowers make perfect landing pads and there is a lot of nectar to eat. The plants grow easily from seeds dropped in the garden, so you can dig up new plants and share them.

Sedum

(sun or part shade)

There are several different kinds of sedum, which have thick, juicy leaves and pretty flowers. The big types of sedum have leaves that, if you are careful and don't break the skin, can be mashed up on the inside and blown up like little balloons. Butterflies love sedum!

Yarrow

(sun)

Yarrow, sometimes called by its Latin name "achillea," has been grown for many, many centuries. Colonists used its fern-like leaves as bandages. The small white, yellow, or pink flowers are formed in tight circles like little colorful pancakes.

Beautiful Bulbs

Bulbs are a little different from other flowers. They can live for many years, sprouting leaves and flowers part of the year, then "dying down" to UNDERGROUND plant parts (which are often thick and fleshy), and coming back up the next year. An onion is a bulb that we can eat. A lot of plants that grow from underground plant parts are not REAL bulbs, but gardeners plant them the same way and sometimes even CALL them bulbs. A crocus is really a "corm" and a dahlia is a "tuber."

Many bulbs and bulb-like plants have really beautiful FLOWERS, but some are grown just for their pretty leaves. Some grow NEW little bulbs around the old ones, and you can dig them up to plant in other areas of the garden or to share. Some bulbs are easy to grow in pots, but most do BEST when they are planted in good flower bed soil.

Bulbs need:

- Good soil that does not stay wet
- Sun at least most of the day
- Water when they get very dry
- Feeding once or twice a year with plant food
- Tall kinds may fall over and need to be tied to a stick (called "staking")

Most bulbs need VERY little extra water (too much water will make them rot), except those that grow and bloom in the hot summer. Water ONLY if the bulbs are growing or flowering during hot, dry, windy weather. At planting time, mix a very SMALL amount of garden or bulb food in the bottom of the hole. The next year, scatter a very small amount of plant food over the area where they are planted. The best "rule of thumb" for planting bulbs is to plant them TWICE as deep as they are big around. Big bulbs should be planted deeper than little bulbs. In fact, you can plant little bulbs ABOVE bigger ones, for an interesting flower combination!

Amaryllis
(sun, or indoors in a pot)

Big, round amaryllis bulbs grow even in a pot indoors! Long leaves come up first, then a thick stem that grows a half-inch or more a day, topped with gigantic trumpet-shaped flowers. Let them dry out and die down after flowering, and they will re-sprout later.

Bluebells
(sun or shade)

Sometimes called "wood hyacinth," this old-fashioned bulb will spread even in shady gardens. It has thin leaves and spikes of blue, pink, purple, or white bell-shaped flowers. Spanish bluebells do best in southern areas, fragrant English bluebells in northern regions.

Caladium
(shade or part sun)

These big-leaf plants with colorful stripes and speckles of red, green, and white, are not true bulbs—they are tubers. They grow best in hot weather, so start their bumpy tubers indoors in pots, then plant them outside when the weather gets hot. They can be dug up and saved over the winter, but it's easier to just plant new ones every year.

Crocus
(sun or part shade)

Little crocuses are the start of spring—sometimes they even bloom in the snow. They don't cost much at all, and are very easy to plant. You can put them where summer plants will come up later, or even in the lawn. A crocus is a corm, not a true bulb.

Daffodil
(sun or part shade)

There are many different kinds of daffodils (sometimes called by their Latin name "narcissus"). There are tiny, six-inch-tall daffodils, and tall, big-flowered ones. The leaves need plenty of sunlight to form next year's flowers inside the bulbs, so don't cut the leaves off too soon or braid them. Wait until the leaves are mostly yellow, about two-thirds their length or more, before removing them.

Dahlia
(sun)

Not a true bulb but a tuber, dahlias make some of the biggest flowers of all—sometimes the size of dinner plates! They need warm soil, and staking to keep them from falling over under the weight of their own flowers. They are great for lots and lots of easy flowers.

Dutch Iris
(sun)

These small bulbs make really beautiful flowers in the spring. They are great for bouquet flowers and are tall enough to mix with other bulbs and spring flowers in the garden. They can also be grown in a pot with pansies on a sunny porch.

Elephant Ears
(sun or part shade)

These giants of the bulb world have leaves that look exactly like their name—huge, heart-shaped green or sometimes purple leaves sprout from great big tubers. In northern regions they have to be dug up, dried, and saved over the winter indoors.

Garlic
(sun)

The most famous flavoring for soups, chili, spaghetti, and other dishes can be grown in your own garden! Peel small "cloves" from a head of garlic, plant in good dirt in the fall, and they will grow plants and even soft-ball-size flowers the next spring.

Gladiolus
(sun)

Not a true bulb, the flat, round, knobby corms can be planted as soon as the dirt warms in the spring. They have long, sword-like leaves and tall spikes of very beautiful flowers—perfect for bouquets. They usually need staking to keep from falling over.

Grape Hyacinth
(sun or part shade)

This bulb is small and multiplies to form groups, with lots of thin, grassy leaves. When they bloom, there are many short stalks covered with clusters of blue flowers that look like tiny grapes. They are one of the first plants to come up in the late winter and begin blooming.

Hyacinth
(sun)

These fat bulbs can be planted in the garden, in pots, or even in a vase or glass filled with gravel and water just touching the bottom of the bulb. They flower with thick stalks of very sweet smelling red, white, blue, pink, or yellow flowers.

Tiger Lily
(sun or part shade)

This bulb has been grown in gardens for a very, very long time. Tiger lily gets really tall, with many narrow leaves all the way up the stalk. In summer it is topped with orange flowers spotted with brown freckles. It needs really good soil, and sometimes needs staking so it won't fall over. Where the leaves meet the stem, small brown "bulbils" will form, drop to the ground, and grow into new plants.

Tulip
(sun)

This is one of the most popular bulbs to bloom in the spring. Mix with pansies and other bulbs in the garden or in pots. Tulips need cold weather to bloom well—in southern regions put them in the refrigerator for six weeks before planting.

Great Potted Plants

Everyone LOVES to grow plants in pots, indoors or out. Some have really pretty leaves, some have flowers, and some are very strange and fun to grow. Some grow OUTSIDE in the sunshine or shade, and others need to be brought INDOORS when the weather gets cold. Plastic pots are the easiest to use, but you can also grow plants in clay pots, metal cans (with holes in the bottom), even a BOOT or an old tire! You can use anything that holds potting soil and has holes in the bottom to let out extra water. You can make a fun COLLECTION of different pots and different plants!

Potted plants need:

- Pots or other containers
- Good potting soil
- Sun or bright light
- Water when they get dry
- Feeding every few weeks with potted-plant fertilizer

Since they are in pots, these plants really need your help to get everything they need. Plants in pots need a FLUFFY kind of soil. Garden soil gets muddy or is very hard when it dries, so it is best to buy good potting soil from a garden center. If you want, you can add some compost to it to make it even better. Some plants

need A LOT of sunlight—put them in a window that faces south or west where the sun shines a long time. Others need bright light but not hot sunlight directly on their leaves, so put them NEAR a window, but not right in the sunshine. VERY few plants will grow across the room from a window, so if you don't have a good window, use a bright lamp near the plant.

Most plants in pots need to be watered EVERY week, sometimes more often if they are in the sun and dry out. If you let a potted plant dry out for too long, it will wilt and die. If you keep it wet all the time, roots will get mushy and die. Water potted plants two times—once with just a little water to make the potting soil swell up like a SPONGE, and another time a few minutes later to help water soak in well. If any water runs onto the floor, clean it up QUICKLY!

Airplane Plant
(part shade)

This indoor plant can live for many years. It has long leaves, sometimes with white stripes, and long, skinny stems that hang down with little plants on the ends. Cut off some of the little ones to plant in other small pots, and share with family and friends!

Aloe
(sun)

Juicy, pointed leaves with little points along the edges make this a scary-looking plant, but it doesn't stick you like a cactus. If you ever scrape your elbow or knee or burn yourself, spread a little juice from a cut leaf over the hurt area, and it will be like a medicine and make you feel better!

Asparagus Fern
(sun or part shade)
The light green fronds of this plant look a lot like a fern, but it's in the lily family. It grows best on a sunny porch or in a sunny window in the winter. Sometimes its leaves turn yellow, but if you cut them off, the plant will grow more. Use it as a plant-friend for other potted plants

Cactus
(sun)
There are many, many kinds of little cactus plants to grow in small pots that you keep on a sunny windowsill. Some have thorns and some do not, and many have very beautiful flowers. Make a collection of different kinds—but remember, they are cactuses (which come from very dry parts of the world like deserts) and do not like to be watered a lot! Let them get dry sometimes.

Chinese Evergreen
(part shade)

This is one tough plant! It does not like hot sun, so keep it inside near a window and water it when it gets dry. It likes company, so put its pot near bigger plants like a rubber tree. You can root pieces of the stem in a jar of water.

Hens and Chicks
(sun)

Several plants are called hens and chicks because the main plant makes small new plants all around it. This plant grows almost like a cactus—it likes to be in a very sunny window and watered only when it gets very dry. It's sometimes called ghost plant because it's so white. When the fat leaves of this plant fall off, stick them a little ways into potting soil with the stem end down, and they will sprout new plants!

Ivy
(part shade)
There are many different kinds of ivy you can grow. Some have big leaves, some have tiny pointed leaves, and some have light-green or white spots. Grow them in a little shade and water them often. Try training one to grow up a wire made into a heart or other shape!

Pencil Cactus
(sun or part shade)
This funny-looking plant with skinny round stems is not really a cactus, because it has no thorns and the juice inside the stems is white and sticky. For this plant, photosynthesis happens in the green stems more than in the tiny leaves. Grow in a sunny window. Pieces of stems can root easily in potting soil if you do not keep them too wet.

Philodendron
(part shade)

There are many different kinds of philodendron, which come from tropical jungles. Some have great big leaves, some are smaller, and some even grow like vines with heart-shaped leaves. All of them grow best near sunny windows but not in the hot sun, and all like to be watered regularly.

Ribbon Plant
(sun or part shade)

This skinny plant has lots of thin leaves with green and white stripes. It is very easy to grow in bright light and with as much water as you want to give it. Its stem is easy to root in potting soil or a jar of water, and the plant can be grown in a terrarium.

Rubber Tree
(sun or part shade)

This plant gets REALLY big with tall stems and big leaves! It will grow for many years if you keep it near a sunny window and let it get a little dry between watering times. If it gets too tall, cut off the stem about halfway down and it will sprout new branches.

Snake Plant
(part shade, shade)

African jungles have this plant all over the ground! There are different kinds with long or short leaves, some with yellow stripes. Keep this plant in the shade—never in a sunny window—and water only when it gets really dry. Pieces of leaves will root in potting soil but don't keep them wet.

Super Shrubs

Every good garden has a few shrubs (often called "bushes") that grow slowly but live a LONG time—like trees. Their trunks, stems, and branches get bigger every year. Once they get started, they are REALLY easy to grow, and will give you something to watch from year to year. Many shrubs have flowers for just a very short time in the spring or summer, and some have colorful and interesting leaves. For an ALL-YEAR garden, plant shrubs, perennials, annuals, bulbs, and lots of other plants in the same area.

Shrubs need:

- Room to grow
- Good soil that does not stay wet
- Sun at least most of the day
- Water when they get very dry
- Feeding once every year or two with plant food
- Their branches pruned when they get too big

Shrubs will be around for a LONG, long time, so plant them right. The best shrubs are happy in nearly any kind of soil, as long as their roots can grow SIDEWAYS. Gardeners usually add just a little compost, old leaves, or potting soil to their garden dirt, and the shrubs do well after that. Dig a wide hole—WIDE is more important than deep—then spread the roots of your new shrub out a little. Plant them so the TOPS of their roots are level with the soil around them in your garden, but cover the roots with a little extra dirt. Finally, water the plants really well and put a couple of inches of mulch over the root area.

Blueberry

(sun)

Sweet blueberries picked right off a shrub in your own garden are the very best! Blueberry plants need a little extra planting care, but have pretty flowers, then berries, then beautiful red leaves in the fall.

Butterfly Bush

(sun)

This plant is called butterfly bush for a good reason—butterflies hang onto the flowers as if they were made of sugar. Big plants with all-summer pink, purple, or white flowers need to have a few branches cut back every year or they will get too big for your garden.

Conifers
(sun)

Evergreen shrubs give your other plants something to grow around, and also something for you to enjoy in the winter when there are not many flowers. Plant two or three small kinds—called dwarf conifers.

Easter Egg Bush
(sun or shade)

Every spring you will see these in other gardens, so why not put one in your own? You just hang plastic Easter eggs from strings on your shrubs. You can also make a bottle tree or a CD tree.

Rose
(sun)

Some roses are hard even for grownups to grow. But there are a lot of "shrub roses" that flower all spring, summer, and fall, without a lot of trouble. There are also miniature roses that are smaller, with little leaves and flowers. Some of these can be used like annuals, and you can get new ones every year.

Rose of Sharon
(sun or part shade)

This big shrub makes great big cup-shaped flowers of white, pink, red, purple, or even blue all summer, then drops its leaves in the fall. Small plants called "suckers" grow around the bottom and can be dug up and planted somewhere else or shared with friends.

Soft-Tip Yucca
(sun or part shade)
Yucca looks mean, but there are soft-tip kinds that grow really well in flower beds to give you something to look at all season while your flowers come and go. They also have tall spikes of white flowers in the summer and fall. Stick pieces of egg cartons on the leaves!

Wildlife Plants
Many shrubs are good for wildlife, particularly birds. They can be used for places to make nests or hide from danger, and some have berries the birds like to eat. If you want wildlife in your garden, be sure to plant a few shrubs. To be a good habitat, a garden needs lots of different kinds of plants. The more types of plants you have, the more types of creatures will want to visit or live there.

For Parents & Teachers

"No great thing is created suddenly, any more than a bunch of grapes or a fig. If you tell me that you desire a fig, I answer you that there must be time. Let it blossom, then bear fruit, then ripen."

—Epictetus (second century C.E.)

So Much to Learn—Such Short Attention Spans!

How many times have my wife and I asked our two children after school what they learned that day, and got "Nothin'" for a reply? We know they were bombarded with lots of new information, but they simply could not identify personally with much of it, did not have time to absorb it all, or were not engaged by it to the point of wanting to share it with us. Childhood is fleeting, with young people growing up too quickly, and constantly moving on to bigger things. We share what we can, but find that—for better or worse—there are endless opportunities (and distractions) in their explorations of their surroundings, and interactions with friends.

Some parents and teachers have trouble getting started gardening with youth, or continuing with projects when their kids are ready to move into higher levels of learning. This chapter deals with guidelines for teaching our young students through the myriad avenues of the natural world, and for finding resources to help you. Scattered through this section are ideas, tips, insights, and other tidbits on involving all your child's senses and learning needs. A special section points you to some of the best resources for support and help. Check them all out, then choose which ones to help your child or students navigate.

First Things First

As happens all too often, well-meaning parents and highly motivated teachers who want to install a "kid's garden" or outdoor classroom run into problems with planning, funding, maintenance, and time conflicts. The result can be a messy, boring workplace that misses its mark by being used by too few teachers and students. With a few guidelines—and not a lot of money—every home garden or school can have a safe, interesting space for kids where their best interests can be stimulated.

A Bit of History

Less than a century ago, children's gardening education was an exercise in "production horticulture"—hands-on instruction about growing plants for food, fun, or profit. Lately, it has swung towards "environmental education" which places an emphasis on understanding general concepts about the environment. These two schools of thought sometimes seem to compete with each other, when in fact elements of both can be easily combined.

Few schools have actual gardens, because gardening is simply not in the curriculum—at least not like math, science, language, history, geography, music, and art. Because of heavy workloads and hectic schedules, every single activity in an outdoor classroom must have a valid connection to the teachers' clearly stated curriculum, or it simply won't work for long.

Yet, the fact is people learn best through a variety of experiences. A simple butterfly garden can be used to teach not only the relationship between insects and plants, but also how to plan, design, plant, maintain, and use the site for a wide variety of topics that include not only math and science but also language arts, history, geography, art, and more. But growing flowers or herbs or vegetables can also teach lifelong skills that include interpersonal experiences with other people.

Heavy Stuff

There are lots of ways we learn, and, even in the garden, teaching should take advantage of as many of them as possible. Here are some "heavy" discussions, treated very simply, which can offer insights into how children learn—and give you a few clues for teaching.

Multiple Intelligences

Ever notice how most kids are naturally better at doing some things than others, like drawing, math, organizing, or getting along with other children? Maybe they are not as good at some subjects in school but they seem to excel in other ways. Howard Gardner, a Harvard University psychology professor, has proven what many teachers and parents already suspected, that people are smart in different ways. His classifications for different kinds of intelligences include:

- **Linguistic Intelligence** (word smart)
- **Logical-Mathematical Intelligence** (number/reasoning smart)
- **Spatial Intelligence** (picture smart)
- **Body-Kinesthetic Intelligence** (body smart)
- **Musical Intelligence** (music smart)
- **Interpersonal Intelligence** (people smart)
- **Intrapersonal Intelligence** (self smart)
- **Naturalist Intelligence** (nature smart)

The task of parents and teachers is to realize each child is a unique blend of intelligences. We need to make the best use of their natural skills and abilities and help them develop those in which they are less apt. The best gardens provide opportunities for students to utilize their natural intelligences and develop their latent ones.

An outdoor classroom activity might be used to enhance each student's natural intelligence by allowing Linguistic students to write descriptions of plants; Logical-Mathematical students could work on the cost of projects; Spatial students could decide on the arrangement and spacing of plants;

Body-Kinesthetic students could test and evaluate different techniques for planting or build a pallet fence; Musical students could design musical instruments made from natural materials; Interpersonal students could serve as teachers or guides for visitors; Intrapersonal students might be stimulated by helping design spaces in the garden for students to spend time reflecting or studying; and the Naturalist student might help identify climate-appropriate plants for the garden.

Using Environmental Education to Improve Grades

There is a teaching technique that has been found to improve students' standardized test scores in all subjects, reduce discipline problems (as reported by principals) and improve teacher satisfaction. This technique is called Environment As an Integrating Context, or EIC™, developed by the State Education and Environment Roundtable, or SEER (www.seer.org). SEER is a cooperative endeavor of state departments of education, that works to enhance student achievement, improve K-12 instructional practices, and help schools achieve their improvement goals by implementing the EIC Model™, a system of educational practices developed and copyrighted by SEER. The EIC Model™ interconnects "best practices" in education into an instructional tapestry that improves student achievement by using local natural and community surroundings as a context for learning.

There are many ways to use integrated instruction. Start by involving the student in brainstorming a "laundry list" of questions, problems, projects, and issues in which they are interested. Students progress by formulating a theme statement in the form of a question that will guide their problem solving activity. For example, "If the world is heating up, what crops might grow better?" or "How much can I reduce my family's grocery bills by growing vegetables on the back porch?" "Why should we attract butterflies to the garden?" "What continents do our favorite flowers and food come from?"

Once the student identifies an area he or she is personally interested in, your role is to help the student find resources and references; help develop the necessary skills and begin experimenting; and last, but certainly not least, make sure that curriculum mandates can be covered in the process.

Basic Design Considerations

Curriculum needs aside, there are a few design features found in most successful school/youth gardens around the country: They were developed during a planning workshop for the Kids' Garden at Epcot® in Walt Disney World® in Florida. Note: While children should be involved in as many aspects of design as possible, EVERY consideration must be given to make the area SAFE (physical hazards include sharp edges, changes in elevation, water features, bee stings, poisonous plants and seeds, etc.), and very LOW MAINTE-NANCE. These two factors CANNOT be overstated!

- "Special space" sense of enclosure, including walls and kid-sized, kid-designed entry; security
- Access to water (with a hard surface to keep feet dry) and electricity (with a "ground-fault interrupter circuit" for safety)
- Firm walkways (for wet weather and for access by the disabled)
- Teaching area (classroom setting, partially walled from rest of garden), with shaded seating that stays dry
- Roomy potting bench, and tool and equipment storage (can even double as seating)
- Signs, charts, maps, other teaching tools, outdoor erasable chalkboard
- Raised beds and varied, large containers
- Weather station (rain gauge, thermometer, wind sock, sundial, etc.)
- Water garden (usually small, with easy access for experiments)
- Vertical structures (for vines, banners, art, sense of enclosure)
- Smaller enclosed areas for special lessons (composting, plant propagation, private student counseling, visitors' viewing area)
- Varying elevations (may incorporate a tunnel, slide, bridge, etc.)
- Lots of color, texture, sound, and other sensory considerations
- Wildlife area (bird feeders, birdhouses, butterfly plants—non-bee!—etc.)
- Art (multi-media, can be incorporated in all the other design features)

- Widely varying plants to fit curriculum needs (beyond mere production purposes)—a FEW examples would be plants that are historic, fast growing, fragrant, attractive to wildlife (bird and butterfly), edible (herbs and vegetables), related to geography (plants native to North America, Africa, South America, Asia, etc.), shade loving, economic (cotton, corn, etc.)

There are many other considerations, but these are commonly found in successful gardens both large and small. Other learning opportunities to include in the garden would be:

- Appeal to ALL the senses—and spark curiosity, too.
- Provide LOTS of changing variety through ALL the seasons.
- Show what things are needed by plants to grow.
- Include lots of "hard" features (art, benches, arbors, etc.).
- Teach that gardening is fun, not just work.
- Provide for peer teaching—have kids show things to other kids.

Involve all the senses when teaching—the possibilities are endless. Hearing alone, and even seeing, is less effective than when combined with touching, smelling, or tasting. As John Guyton, one of America's top youth environmental educators puts it, "If you are teaching about Leif Ericson and his discovering Vineland, you'd jolly well better have grapes for the students to be eating!"

Beyond simply having herbs and vegetables for eating and smelling, include different walkway materials for "feet feeling," wind chimes and student-made musical instruments, poetry readings and discussions, a labyrinth to run through. Even a simple, heavy, knotted rope hanging from a (sturdy) tree limb can stimulate imagination and play. Also, keep a few old logs nearby for exploration—the mushy feel of moist, rotting wood can lead to amazing discoveries.

Tips for Working with Kids in a Garden

Once you have made a place for gardening and exploration, and have found the time, there are a number of things you should consider in making the experience more engaging for children.

- Children have short attention spans—give them lots of different activities from which to choose.
- Instant gratification is crucial—plants take time to grow, so have kids make projects to keep their attention going over the weeks.
- Show children what you want them to do—don't just tell them.
- It's okay to get dirty—that's what soap and water are for!
- Teach them to respect all of nature, and not be cruel to critters.
- Make sure there are enough seeds, tools, etc. to go around.
- Follow up each activity with a review or question-and-answer time.
- Have kids write things down or draw pictures to hang on the wall or refrigerator.
- Encourage quiet children to talk in small groups, not large ones.
- Color, color, color! And textures!
- Take advantage of existing features—have children decorate a water faucet, chain link fence, rain gutter downspouts, garden gates, walkways (using chalk, of course), walls, telephone poles (make "palm leaves" from cardboard or wood), logs—there are numerous possible ideas!

Failure Recovery

Stuff often goes wrong in gardens. Plants die—even under the care of garden experts!—and bugs, slugs, rabbits, and deer often eat more than their fair share. Heavy rains, hot summers, and occasional vandalism all enter our lives at some point.

Where better to learn how to deal with frustration and failure, and to talk about it, than in the safety of a garden? Use such situations to help children rationalize and work out a healthy plan for coping with the inevitable downsides of life.

How to Use This Book

Any given plant, project, or combination of plants and projects can be used to teach a number of subjects and communicate a variety of ideas. For example, a cactus can initiate a discussion of deserts; compared to a daisy it offers the chance to look at plant parts and adaptation. A garden of drought-tolerant plants (such as yucca, rosemary, and moss rose) offers the chance to talk about weather and soil (as well as being easy to maintain). A desert terrarium project can lead to a discussion of habitats, particularly if a terrarium of tropical plants is also made as contrast. Choose a plant or project and see how many ideas you can communicate with it, or choose a topic and find plants and projects to illustrate. There are really infinite possibilities.

Learning from Plants

The plants in this book have all been selected according to their ease of growing, especially by children and less garden-experienced parents or teachers in small-scale gardens. Obviously they can be used to illustrate basic elements of science curricula, such as parts of plants, adaptation, pollination, reproduction, photosynthesis, transpiration, and plant growth. They can also be used for teaching about such larger ideas as wildlife, the senses, habitats, nutrition, weather, sociology, history, and geography.

Many homes and schools have at least some outdoor garden space available. But there are also opportunities in smaller spaces, such as plants in containers. Plants can be grown indoors, on a windowsill, under a grow light, or on a porch or stoop. A teacher or parent can be the initiator and provide the plants, a child can be taken to a garden center and allowed to choose his or her own plants, or the plants can be propagated. Growing plants from seeds can also be a fascinating and rewarding experience, for both children and adults.

As an example of how a plant can be used as a teaching tool, take bee balm.

- Identify all the plant parts (if it's in a pot you can even take it out and look at the roots).
- Look closely at the flowers and talk about what sorts of creatures they attract (bees, butterflies, hummingbirds), why that happens (pollination), and how they do it (color, scent). Why is it mutually beneficial for insects and birds to visit flowers?
- Discuss how the plant got the name "bee balm."
- Look at the stem and note that it is square, which indicates that it is in the mint family (talk about what other plants are in the same family—mint, coleus). Many common weeds (probably growing in the lawn or playground) are also relatives—ground ivy, henbit, purple dead nettle.
- Rub the leaves and enjoy the scent. Also bring in herbal tea with bee balm in it and let the child or children sample it.
- Bee balm is also called "Oswego tea," for the Native American tribe. This offers the chance to talk about herbs, herbal medicine, Native American culture, and nature as both a grocery store and drugstore for Native Americans and early colonists.
- Discuss where bee balm is found growing in the wild and what it would need to be happy in a garden. Since it is native to North America, talk about other plants that grow wild in the region, and plants from other countries.

With this one plant you can cover biology, history, ecology, social science, and language. Any given plant can have similar opportunities for teaching.

Mix 'Em Up!

While a single plant can be a great teaching tool, shrubs, bulbs, annuals, perennials, vegetables, herbs, and potted plants can also be grown in combination, which does several things:

- Looks great and provides a lot of texture and color in a small space
- Makes it easier to plant and replant through several seasons

- Requires less maintenance than plants scattered all over the place
- Reduces pest problems by creating a baffling "target" for pests
- Helps make losing a plant here and there less noticeable
- Provides diversity, which increases the chances of attracting wildlife

A garden with many types of plants is more interesting, more colorful, and more full of living things. Choose plants that need the same growing conditions, and allow each of them enough space to reach their ultimate height and width. Take stock of such logistical issues as the location of a spigot for watering (new plants and plants under drought stress will need regular water); accessibility for bringing in plants, mulch, and other materials; and foot traffic patterns (planting in an obvious pathway will only lead to damaged plants).

Eat What You Grow

While growing plants for their beauty or appeal to wildlife is fertile ground for teaching, edible plants can also be grown. Healthy eating starts at home! It has been shown over and over that kids are more likely to eat healthy if they grow it themselves—and this can translate into lifelong good habits.

Radishes are not quite as fun to eat as bananas, and raw bell peppers are not always appetizing to kids accustomed to pepperoni pizza—but these two vegetables grow easily, and what the children learn in the process about the simplicity of growing a few plants in a small space can expand to many other plants as they grow up and start gardens of their own. Once they gain confidence growing one plant, it will encourage them to grow others.

It is not easy to grow food during some parts of the school year (particularly over the winter), but having a garden area for edible plants can still be beneficial. Raised beds that drain well and warm faster in the spring, and are part of a more intimate garden setting (as opposed to being stuck way out in the yard, away from the house or garden hose), can help give a head start to growing things in the spring. Plus, kids can more easily plant, water, and care for small, intensively planted areas, and replant quickly as seasons change. Herbs can also be used to carry an edible garden through the down times.

Using the Projects

How can you use the projects in this book to teach a wide variety of topics? There are several ways to go about it. Going through the process of making something can be interesting in and of itself, and learning can occur on a subconscious level. You never know what sort of thing will strike a chord in a child, or remain as a fond memory that he or she will follow up on later in life. Or simple, linear connections can be made between projects and topics—keeping the exploration process low-key and not too academic. But there is also the opportunity for deeper discovery, moving out in larger and larger circles to include a myriad of subjects. You can start with either the subject or the project—it's just two ways of looking at the same thing. And you can research the idea further through other projects, books, the Internet, magazines, or videos as seems appropriate.

Making Connections

One approach is to take a SUBJECT and explore it through one or multiple projects. For example, to illustrate that decay is a part of the cycle of life, you can start with the very simple Grow Some Mold project (page 62), expand on the idea using the Indoor Worm Box (pages 64–65), then (if you have the space for it) move to a larger project with Compost (pages

32–33). You can also relate the subject to recycling things that resist decay, using such projects as the CD Tree (page 53), Tire Sculptures (page 48), Milk Jug Bird Feeder (page 22), and Aluminum Can Chimes (page 27).

Or you can choose a PROJECT and see how many subjects you can explore through it. Sometimes a project can have many levels of exploration possible, covering not only science but other subjects as well. For example, the Dinosaur Puzzle (page 49) can be used to examine the use of different materials (cardboard, wood), spatial skills (designing a three-dimensional structure using two-dimensional pieces), art, history (when did dinosaurs live?), and even building and architecture. You can use the Dinosaur Puzzle project to initiate a visit to an art museum to see other sculptures, or a natural history museum, particularly one that includes fossil skeletons.

If you want to add related projects, here are a few ideas:

- Have the children draw a grid over a picture of a dinosaur, then draw a chalk grid on the driveway or parking lot, and use the two grids to sketch a life-size picture on the parking lot (depending on the size of your driveway, it is probably easier if you choose a smaller dinosaur, rather than the giant *Tyrannosaurus rex*).
- Have them paint a time line on a long piece of paper, showing what animals and plants lived at different points along it, or paint a mural of different dinosaurs and other creatures.
- For fun, make a list of incorrect elements in Barney or other "dinosaur" cartoons (Could dinosaurs talk and dance? Did they stand on two legs? Does it make sense for the Flintstones to have a dinosaur as a pet?).

Problem Solving

Another approach is to take a project, pose questions, and seek answers. According to the mantra of Dr. John Guyton, one of our country's leading environmental education specialists, "It all boils down to thinking about questions, problems, and issues." Take a project—*any one of them*—and apply a topic (history, math, linguistics, art, science, geography, history, music, etc.), then think about questions, problems, and issues. You'll be surprised at how many you can come up with.

For the subjects of decay and compost you could present such problems/questions as:

- Weigh or measure by volume the amount of material put in the compost, then the amount of material taken out for use (hint: this would be easier using the Indoor Worm Box project as a miniature compost bin).
- How much compost would it take to cover the front yard, the driveway, or a small garden bed (lots of math here)?
- Where do all the leaves go when the garbage truck hauls them off?
- If you put together all the bags of leaves created in one town, would this take up a lot of space?
- If one bag of leaves were composted, how much of a garden area would this benefit?

If you want to take the compost idea further, there are other projects that can be utilized. The "bio-tower" is a different type of compost project, with a recycling system. Take two soda bottles; cut one in half, cut the very bottom

off of the other, and punch holes in the bottle caps. Put compost and a few worms in the bottomless bottle and invert it into the bottom half of the other bottle. Invert the top half-bottle into the bottomless bottle and put potting soil and a plant in it. As you water the plant on top it will filter down through the compost. Use the nutrient-rich water collected at the bottom of the structure to water the plant on top, and so on. This is an easy way to demonstrate several things in a very small space.

It's possible to use a project to cover nearly every subject in the curriculum. For the Water Gardening project (page 50) you can pose such questions as:

- How much water does the pond hold? How much evaporates daily? (Math)
- Use split bamboo or other "channels" to move water from various heights, and explain gravity. How can you make the water move faster or slower through the channels? (Physics)
- Examine different types of living things associated with ponds, such as plants, insects, amphibians, aquatic animals, algae, and microscopic creatures. How do they affect each other? (Biology)
- Look at a map of your area that shows waterways. Do you live near a "watershed" (river basin), lake, pond, or stream? Notice how the waterways are connected. How do you think water affects land, and how does land affect water? If your water garden overflows, how does it affect the area around it? (Geography)
- Research past cultures and find examples of water gardens long ago. Why did they build them? (History)
- Write a poem about the water garden. Find a poem written by a poet about a pond, lake, or stream. What are the words they use to describe water? (Literature)
- Draw and paint dragonflies and water garden plants. Look at various artists' paintings of water and water gardens, such as Monet's water lilies. How does each artist paint water differently? (Art)
- Fill same-size glasses with different amounts of water and tap on them to make tunes. (Music)
- Make a "deer chaser" or a dry gravel pond and discuss Japanese gardens. (Social Studies)

Combining Projects and Plants

In addition to using the plants as teaching tools and using the projects, there are numerous combinations of plants and projects. For example, while the Wildlife Garden project would include many different kinds of plants to teach about attracting butterflies (zinnias), providing caterpillars with necessary food (fennel, parsley), and helping birds find nesting places (shrubs), it can also be combined with the Water Gardening project and the Compost project to expand the opportunities for "teachable moments" and maintain a child's interest through the year.

Using containers and having children create and add "hard features" such as a CD tree, scarecrow, or other artwork, creates instant visual gratification while plants take their time growing, plus providing year-round interest.

Storytelling

Some elements can be combined to create perfect situations for storytelling. An easy example is the "Three Sisters" myth in which Native Americans explained

why for many centuries they grew corn, beans, and squash or pumpkins together in hills. The corn shaded the squash and provided a climbing place for beans, which fed the soil and enriched it for the squash and corn. This ancient practice provided nearly perfect companions for growing—and for complete nutrition as well!

The Vine Teepee project (page 58) can be used as a tie-in since it provides storytelling and reading opportunities about Native Americans, what kinds of structures they lived in, what they ate, how they traveled and traded, and so on. Growing bean vines on the teepee provides additional interest.

Appealing to the Senses

It is very important that all the senses be stimulated in the garden! This can be used to provoke thoughtful questions, and both plants and projects can keep children occupied with exploring, note taking, and comparisons. Here are just a few possibilities:

- **Sight:** zinnia, celosia, iris, Easy Scarecrow, Weather Station, Potato Bouquet, Plant a Rainbow
- **Taste:** parsley, basil, daylily, thyme, tomatoes, sunflower, Dried Fruit Slices
- **Smell:** basil, four-o'-clocks, mint, garlic, hyacinth, oregano, Compost
- **Touch:** globe amaranth, snapdragon, lamb's ears, conifer shrubs, Water Gardening, Wattle Fence
- **Sound:** gourds, grasses, Aluminum Can Chimes

Rather than limiting a child's understanding of the senses to something tasting, smelling, or feeling "good" or "bad," expand their ways of interpreting their experiences. Mix different herbs separately in butter, spread each mixture on a cracker, and see if the child can taste the subtle differences. Explore the variety of scents present in such things as garlic, roses, and carnations,

or even different types of mint or scented geraniums. Touch different objects or plants (even blindfolded) and find words to describe the varying textures, like "downy," "smooth," "grainy," "rough," "prickly," and "papery."

Make wind chimes from different materials and consider, if the chimes were singing would they be a soprano voice or a bass (or are they singing off-key!). Make a bouquet of all pink (or yellow or red) flowers (using different types of plants), or collect a variety of leaves (after all, green is a color too!). Are all the pinks or all the greens the same color? Learning to "see" in a new way makes the world much more interesting and exciting, and can lead to inspiration and further exploration.

Resource Organizations That Can Help—A Lot

There is no need to "reinvent the wheel" when it comes to working with children and gardening—there are many organizations located in all parts of the country geared up to help, often for free, offering to train both you and your children in or out of school through workshops, tours, projects, and even Internet sites.

Most botanic gardens now have—or are planning—some sort of youth garden, or at least have seasonal classes. At the very least they are great sources for inspiration and even plants and supplies.

There are quite a few safe, easy-to-navigate Internet sites with information, tips, projects, and supplies for children who want to garden. A word search will come up with plenty, but a great start is the National Gardening Association (www.garden.org) and its fun, link-filled children's gardening website (www.kidsgardening.com). It is commercial, but very helpful.

Also have children do word searches for general terms like "worm composting" and "garden poetry" and "kid's garden projects" and the like. Be sure to supervise general word searches—there's no telling what can pop up these days!

Here are a few of the most-used non-profit organizations that have in-depth websites specifically for youth gardening, whether in school or at home. Have kids look them up on the Internet, and see what they have to offer.

American Horticultural Society

The American Horticultural Society (www.ahs.org), one of the oldest national gardening organizations in the country, considers the children's garden one of the strongest trends in gardening. It helps children develop social skills, enhances school curricula, brings families together, and creates an awareness of the link between nature and our food, clothing, and shelter. Children's gardens replace the free exploration of the natural world that no longer occurs in today's era of TVs, video games, and concern over safety.

In 1998, many notable leaders in the field of youth garden education joined AHS in creating a National Children and Youth Garden Advisory Panel. In support of the mission of AHS to educate and inspire people of all ages to become successful and environmentally responsible gardeners by advancing the art and science of horticulture, the panel proposed the following plan to address the specific opportunities and needs of children and youth gardening:

- To inspire children, youth, and all persons involved in education; to create and use school, home, and public gardens as places of enrichment and delight for all who are young at heart
- To promote an understanding of plants and the important roles they play in our daily lives
- To encourage links and interactions among private and public gardens and teacher education programs that engage teachers in garden-based training

Its Youth Gardening link includes a National Registry of Youth Gardens, links to botanical gardens with children's gardens, dozens of resources, information about youth gardening conferences, and much more.

Master Gardeners

Master Gardeners are trained volunteers working out of county or parish Cooperative Extension Service offices. They usually have current knowledge of local and area youth gardens and opportunities, and often hold classes for kids. Contact them through your county Cooperative Extension Service, or by going to the American Horticultural Society's web page (www.ahs.org) and clicking on the Master Gardener link.

Junior Master Gardeners

The Junior Master Gardener program is an international youth gardening program of the University Cooperative Extension network, correlated to state teaching standards. Its mission is to "grow good kids" by igniting a passion for learning, success, and service through unique gardening education, using independent and group learning experiences. Students use what they have learned to be of service to others. Examples of service projects initiated by JMG groups include: growing produce to donate to food banks, community beautification projects, and class businesses generating funds for local charities. The JMG site (www.jmgkids.org) has links to many state university gardening sites.

4-H Youth Programs

Every county or parish has access to a university-trained 4-H Youth Agent who can help you with training materials, workshops, or even an after-school club. The web page for your state Extension Service has links to gardening, environmental, and other youth educational programs. Some states have well-established children's gardens with summer camps.

Project Learning Tree

Project Learning Tree® (www.plt.org), a program of the American Forest Foundation, is a broad-based program for educators and students in Pre-K through grade 12. PLT helps students learn HOW to think, not WHAT to think, about the environment. PLT materials bring the environment into the classroom and students into the environment. The program covers topics ranging from forests, wildlife, and water to community planning, waste management, and energy. It makes correlations to national and state standards in science, social studies, language arts, math, and other subjects, while strengthening critical thinking, team building, and problem solving skills.

157

Project WILD

Project WILD (www.projectwild.org) is another of the most widely used conservation and environmental education programs among educators of students in kindergarten through high school. It is based on the premise that young people and educators have a vital interest in learning about our natural world. The program emphasizes wildlife because of its intrinsic and ecological values, as well as its importance as a basis for teaching how ecosystems function. In the face of competing needs and pressures affecting the quality and sustainability of life on earth, Project WILD addresses the need for human beings to be responsible citizens of our planet.

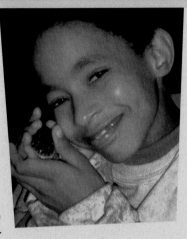

Project WET

Project WET (www.projectwet.org), which stands for Water Education for Teachers, is a nonprofit water education program and publisher for educators and young people ages 5-18. The program facilitates and promotes awareness, appreciation, knowledge, and stewardship of water resources through the dissemination of classroom-ready teaching aids and the establishment of internationally sponsored Project WET programs.

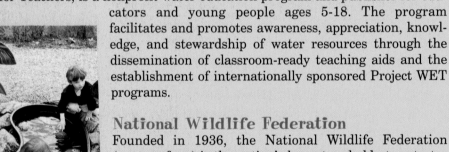

National Wildlife Federation

Founded in 1936, the National Wildlife Federation (www.nwf.org) is the nation's largest and oldest protector of wildlife. With more than four million members and supporters, NWF is committed to educating and empowering people from all walks of life to protect wildlife and habitat for future generations. NWF provides youth educational resources and programs aimed at various age levels from pre-K through high school, newsletters for parents, and newsletters for both formal and non-formal educators who teach science, social studies, and language arts. NWF also provides guidance and certification for backyard and school wildlife habitats.

NOTE: You can contact any native plant or wildflower organization in the U.S. by going to the Lady Bird Johnson Wildflower Center's web page at www.wildflower.org.

Food, Land, and People

Food, Land, and People (www.foodlandpeople.org), established in 1988, is based in the Presidio National Park of San Francisco. Food, Land, and People is a nonprofit organization committed to helping people of all ages better understand the interrelationships among agriculture, the environment, and people of the world, and to make thoughtful choices for the future.

Food, Land, and People's science- and social sciences-based curriculum, *Resources for Learning*, currently serves Pre-K to 12th grade students throughout the United States. The curriculum consists of hands-on lessons, developed and tested by more than a thousand educators. The subjects range from environmental science and stewardship ("Don't Use It All Up!") to human populations and land use issues ("What Will the Land Support?").

American Association of Botanical Gardens and Arboreta

The AABGA is an umbrella organization for public gardens in North America. Not every public garden in the U.S. is a member, but many are. The AABGA website (www.aabga.org) has links to gardens (under Member Gardens) and it is searchable by state or region. Many botanical gardens and similar institutions have children's gardens or children's educational programming available to the public. There are also opportunities for school tours. Check out the websites of public gardens in your area and find out what they have to offer.

Public gardens can be interesting for kids to visit even if there is not a children's garden on site, or a formal children's educational program. There are often herb gardens, water gardens, Japanese gardens, wildflower gardens, and so on that present a wide variety of learning opportunities. If you do not have a space for a garden at home or at school, a public garden can serve as a "borrowed" garden (without the digging and weeding!) for experiencing sights, sounds, scents, and textures. You can see things at a public garden that you are unlikely to find on home ground, and you might even find inspiration for your own garden.

Meet the Author

FELDER RUSHING

is a defender of truth in gardening and is dedicated to educating both children and adults. He raised his two children from the perspective that gardening is natural and easy as well as productive. While studying and teaching in youth gardens on four continents, he helped disadvantaged children build raised bed gardens in South America and Africa. As a member of the National Youth Garden Advisory Committee, the teacher and author of over a dozen gardening books (including another one for kids) helped design the Walt Disney World® Kids' Garden at Epcot® in Florida, and has provided many youth-oriented teacher education programs and hands-on workshops around the country. Working with Master Gardeners, librarians, and schoolteachers, he has personally designed several children's gardens in his home state of Mississippi.

Believing that too many educators and scientists make gardening and environmental education more complicated than need be ("We are daunted, not dumb," he says), Rushing continually uncovers simple lessons to stimulate all the senses and inspire a new generation of gardeners—and their grownups.